NUGGETS OF WISDOM FROM GREAT JEWISH THINKERS:

FROM BIBLICAL TIMES TO THE PRESENT

VALUE INQUIRY BOOK SERIES

VIBS

Volume 14

Robert Ginsberg

Executive Editor

Moses Maimonides (1135-1204). Medallion in the U.S. Capitol, Washington D.C.   Prints and Photographs Division, Library of Congress.

NUGGETS OF WISDOM FROM GREAT JEWISH THINKERS:

From Biblical Times to the Present

William Gerber

Rodopi

Amsterdam - Atlanta, GA 1994

BM
43
.G47
1994

∞™The paper used in this publication meets the minimum requirements of American National Standard for information Sciences - Permanence of Paper for Printed Library Materials, ANSI Z.39.48-1984.

Cover design Chris Kok based on a photograph, ©1984 by Robert Ginsberg, of statuary by Gustav Vigeland in the Frogner Park, Oslo, Norway

ISBN: 90-5183-720-8 (bound)
©Editions Rodopi B.V., Amsterdam - Atlanta, GA 1994
Printed in The Netherlands

OTHER BOOKS BY THE AUTHOR

The Domain of Reality (1946)

American Liberalism (1975; revised edition 1987)

Serenity (1986)

Pathways to a More Satisfying Life (1990)

Editor of

The Mind of India (1967; paperback editions 1977, 1991)

A Philosopher's Harvest; The Philosophical Papers of Isaac Franck (1988)

CONTENTS

FOREWORD BY THE SERIES EDITOR

Dr. William Gerber has mined the richness of thousands of years of Jewish reflection to assemble for us useful and provocative nuggets of wisdom. In a brief yet remarkable exploration, Gerber takes us from the celebrated ancient depths of Judaism through its strong medieval heritage to the troubling times of modern life and death. Continuities of concern are evident as well as fresh twists on old questions. Jewish thought makes its advances in a spiralling fashion, turning around the perduring problems of being human while moving forward into life. A passionate care for humane values underlies much of Jewish thinking and cries out for philosophical recognition.

Gerber has assayed the enormous material of Jewish philosophical and religious thought to set forward outstanding crystallizations. These insights, queries, and proposals are touchstones for the reader who seeks familiarity with Jewish reflection on values. But they are not restricted to historical documentation of one people's past experience, nor is Gerber's effort a contribution to official doctrine or religious apology. Connections will strike the reader between some passages and values held dear by Christianity, Islam, Indian religions, and other spiritual systems, as well as by secular thought.

By careful selection, astute juxtaposition, and gentle commentary, Gerber makes these passages come alive as addressed to all thinking persons who wonder about righteousness in a world of suffering and evildoing, and to all who wonder about their humanity in its relationship to divinity. These nuggets, then, are part of the richness of our own existence as human beings. May we learn from them to grow wise.

Executive Editor
Robert Ginsberg

PREFACE

Jewish prophets, sages, and writers—beginning in Biblical times and continuing to the present—have creatively fashioned expressions of timeless wisdom about how the world operates, how we live, and how we ought to live. These enchanting nuggets of wisdom deserve to be read and re-read, with a view not only to deepening our grasp of the nature of things but also to helping us react in suitable ways to the vicissitudes of life.

In the present volume, I have woven together some of the most gracious of these expressions of wisdom, with the hope that their deployment in a coherent structural framework may be useful to readers who are seekers of basic truths.

In Part Two of this volume, I quote the statement, made in a fourth-century rabbinical work, "At Sinai, the women received and accepted the Decalogue before the men." My comment immediately following that quotation is as follows:

> "The. . . [statement] which you have just read, on the exalted role of women at Sinai, may assuage the disquiet which feminists among my readers may have felt over the repeated use, in my selections, of the word 'men' as referring to all human beings."

In that connection, I hope that my readers will bear in mind that, in many quotations appearing in all four parts of this volume, "men" may be interpreted as applying to all human beings.

I should add that, in quoting noteworthy passages from Jewish wisdom writings, I have occasionally italicized a few words which are not italicized in the published source from which I have taken the passage. I have done so in order to facilitate a quick absorption of the passage's basic thrust.

W.G.

LIST OF ILLUSTRATIONS

ACKNOWLEDGMENTS

Earlier versions of the four parts of this volume were circulated privately, as follows:

Part One, a preliminary text, reproduced from typewritten copy, Washington, 1989.

Parts Two, Three, and Four, privately printed, Washington, 1990, 1991, and 1992, respectively.

*   *   *   *

Credit for Use of
Copyrighted Texts

The kind permission of the following publishers and copyright owners to reprint passages from the books indicated is gratefully acknowledged.

B'nai B'rith International Headquarters (Washington, D.C.), Commission on Continuing Education — Chaim Pearl's translation entitled *Rashi's Commentaries on the Pentateuch* (1970).

Doubleday & Company — *The Dead Sea Scriptures in English Translation*, With Introduction and Notes by Theodore H. Gaster (1956).

Hebrew Publishing Company, P.O. Box 157, Rockaway Beach, NY 11693; all rights reserved — (1) *Maimonides' Mishneh Torah (Yad Hazakah)*, edited and translated by Philip Birnbaum (Hebrew-English edition, copyright 1967); and (2) *The New Treasury of Judaism*, edited by Philip Birnbaum (copyright 1967).

Bernard Lewis — Solomon ibn Gabirol, *The Kingly Crown*, Newly Translated With an Introduction and Notes, by Bernard Lewis (London: Vallentine, Mitchell, 1961).

Penguin Books USA — *The Living Talmud: The Wisdom of the Fathers*, edited by Judah Goldin, copyright 1957 by Judah Goldin, permission granted by Professor Goldin and the New American Library, a division of Penguin Books USA.

Random House — (1) *A Jewish Reader: In Time and Eternity*, edited by Nahum N. Glatzer, translated in part by Olga Marx Perlzweig, copyright 1946 (renewed 1974) and 1961 by Schocken Books, permission granted by Schocken Books, a division of Random House; and (2) *Hammer on Rock: A Short Midrash Reader*, edited by Nahum N. Glatzer, translated by Jacob Sloan, copyright 1948 and 1962 (renewed 1975) by Schocken Books, permission granted by Schocken Books, a division of Random House.

Reconstructionist Press — (1) Mordecai M. Kaplan, *Questions Jews Ask: Reconstructionist Answers* (1956); and (2) *Dynamic Judaism: The Essential Writings of Mordecai M. Kaplan*, edited by Emanuel S. Goldsmith and Mel Scult (1985).

Russell & Volkening (literary agents, representatives of the heirs of Milton Steinberg) — Milton Steinberg, *Anatomy of Faith* (1960).

Yale University Press — *Karaite Anthology: Excerpts from the Early Literature*, translated by Leon Nemoy, copyright 1952 by Yale University Press, renewed 1980 by Leon Nemoy, permission granted by Yale University Press.

Credit for Use of
Copyrighted Pictures

The kind permission of the following sources to print the pictures indicated is gratefully acknowledged.

Leo Baeck Institute, New York, New York; and Photo Archive of the Beit Hatefutsot (Museum of the Diaspora), Tel Aviv, Israel—Picture of Baruch Spinoza.

Photo Archive of the Beit Hatefutsot (Diaspora Museum), Tel Aviv, Israel—Lithographs of an engraving of Moses Maimonides and of a painting of Moses Mendelssohn.

HarperCollins Publishers, New York, New York—Picture of Abraham Isaac Kook, from *The Illustrated History of the Jews*, by Benjamin Mazar, copyrighted 1963 by the Israeli Publishing Institute.

Jewish Theological Seminary, New York—Photograph of Mordecai M. Kaplan.

Jewish National & University Library, Jerusalem, Israel— Picture of Martin Buber.

Rabbi Simon Noveck, Toms River, New Jersey—Picture of Milton Steinberg.

Peter Stein—Photograph of Albert Einstein, from Fred Stein, *World Celebrities in 90 Photographic Portraits* (New York: Dover Publications, copyright 1988 by Peter Stein).

Introduction

THE CORE OF JEWISH WISDOM

Discernible in Jewish wisdom, as expressed in the nuggets displayed in this volume, are several features which, taken individually, are not unique to the Jewish tradition, but, taken together, constitute an integrally woven, recognizable, and indeed unique Jewish contribution to civilization. Among these features, which *together* constitute Jewish wisdom, are several far-reaching moral or spiritual injunctions. I am listing some of them here.

(1) Be humble—especially in moments of success or triumph.

(2) Seriously consider the needs, wants, individuality, and humanity of others in choosing your behavior toward them.

(3) Cherish the ideal of returning good for evil, even if you cannot bring yourself to apply it to everyone always.

(4) Open yourself to the wonders that surround you in daily living.

(5) Imbibe and savor such spirituality, and evidences of divinity, as you can perceive in the world of living and non-living things.

For each of these injunctions which together constitute the essence of Jewish wisdom, I am summarizing below a selection of pertinent nuggets which are quoted more fully in the remainder of this book.

1. Practice Humility

Humility is one of the only three things that God reportedly requires of humans ("what doth the Lord require of thee," asked the prophet Micah, "but to do justly, and to love mercy, and to walk humbly with thy God?").

Moreover three opposites of humility—namely, pride, boasting, and arrogance—were strongly disparaged by sagacious Jewish writers. *Pride* was condemned in the Book of Proverbs as an "abomination" (the book's list of seven abominations included "[a] proud look"). *Boasting* was belittled in the same book ("Boast not thyself of to-morrow"). *Arrogance* was downgraded in the apocryphal book The Wisdom of Solomon ("What did our arrogancy profit us?").

The Jewish ascetic sect which produced the Dead Sea Scrolls about one century before the common era included in its Manual of Discipline an injunction to be humble even when pursuing litigation ("When anyone has a charge against his neighbor, he is to prosecute it . . . humbly").

The post-Biblical rabbis whose reflections on life were recorded in the Talmud gave a *reason* for being humble ("Be of an exceedingly humble spirit, for the end of man is the worm").

The eleventh-century Spanish-Jewish ethicist Bahya ibn Paquda extolled humility in a string of pearly aphorisms which are quoted on several pages of this study. Where the Talmud gave one kind of reason for being humble ("the end of man is the worm"), ibn Paquda gave another kind of reason—a prudential one ("The humble [person] . . . bears troubles with greater *fortitude* than do the proud").

In the twelfth century, Moses Maimonides, evaluating virtues, rated moderation, or the golden mean, on a top rung, *except* as to what he called "lowliness"; that is, humility ("[I]f the interval between haughtiness and complete lowliness be divided into sixty-four parts, one should stand on the sixty-third step").

Moses Hayyim Luzzatto, the eighteenth-century author of *The Way of God*, rated humility *above wisdom* ("[A]ll the wisdom in the world cannot compare with humility").

Finally, humility is one of the few virtues which are so associated with natural virtue as *not to be capable of being commanded*, according to a modern Hasidic master ("If anyone were humble *in order to keep a commandment*, he would never attain to true humility").

2. *Seriously Consider Others*

The injunction to consider the well-being of others appears early in the Bible, in the Book of Leviticus ("[T]hou shalt love thy neighbour as thyself"), and is eloquently emphasized in the Book of Isaiah ("relieve the oppressed, judge the fatherless, plead for the widow, ... deal thy bread to the hungry, ... [and] when thou seest the naked, ... cover him").

The Talmud includes among the attributes of the wise man consideration for the ego of one who is speaking (the wise man "does not break into his fellow's speech").

The Talmud also reports the sage Hillel's famous epitome of the Torah in terms of understanding others' basic aversions as comparable to one's own ("what is hateful to you, do not do to your fellow").

The post-Talmudic commentaries which are known as Midrashim repeatedly urge consideration of the plight of the poor ("More than the householder does for the beggar, the beggar does for the householder"; "When the beggar stands at your door, the Holy One, blessed be He, stands at his right hand").

In Alexandria, Egypt, Philo the Jew praised consideration toward all, in the form of civility ("I will ... behave myself in an affable, and courteous, and conciliatory manner to all men, even if I should obtain the dominion over all the earth").

Bahya ibn Paquada, whose thoughts on humility we quoted above, also wrote on consideration for others (he said that the virtuous person "will not only do good to all men, but he will speak kindly to them and of them").

In our century, Martin Buber cast a new light on the matter of consideration for others. He distinguished between *I – It* relations with another, in which we view the other mainly as a means to the fulfillment of our own purposes, and *I – Thou* relations, in which we reflect our consideration for another by recognizing in the other his or her own individuality ("[W]ithout *It*, man cannot live; but he who lives with *It* alone is not a [whole] man").

Abraham Joshua Heschel, the American civil rights leader and poetic writer on loftiness in living, also lauded the I – Thou relation ("How rarely do we face a person as a person! ... [Yet] the true meaning of existence is experienced in ... meeting a person face to face").

Finally, I cite Albert Einstein, who likewise celebrated considerate treatment of others ("[I]t is plain that we exist for our fellow men").

3. Return Good for Evil

Moses, after handing down the Ten Commandments, supplemented them with a cluster of specific ethical ideals, including Return Good for Evil ("If thou meet thine enemy's ox or his ass going astray, thou shalt surely bring it back to him").

This ideal is imaginatively supported in the Book of Proverbs ("A soft answer turneth away wrath").

Baruch Spinoza, in the seventeenth century, derived the ideal of returning good for evil by a process of reasoning ("He who lives under the guidance of reason endeavours ... to repay his fellow's hatred, ... contempt, etc., with love and nobleness").

Spanning the end of the eighteenth century and the beginning of the nineteenth, a rabbi living in the Ukraine, Nahman of Bratslav, emphasized the acceptance of insults without retaliation ("[L]ife [being] short, ... [h]ow ... can you waste your time on petty quarrels?").

In the nineteenth century, the Hungarian-Jewish philosopher Solomon Ganzfried rejected answering evil with evil ("the just ... hear themselves reviled and answer not").

4. Open Yourself to Wonders

On openness to the wonders that surround us, my best witness is Albert Einstein, who eloquently and often exalted this ideal and declared it to be a characteristic of

Judaism ("There remains ... something *more* in the Jewish tradition, ... namely, a kind of drunken joy and surprise at the beauty and incomprehensible sublimity of this world").

5. Seek and Exemplify Spirituality

Scripture, elaborations of Scripture (in the Talmud and the Midrash), commentaries on Scripture, and compendiums of Scriptural teachings, as well as a vast treasury of rabbinical and philosophical interpretations encompassing Scripture, Judaism, life, and the world, are rich sources of Jewish wisdom about God, spirituality, sacredness, holiness, reverence, and worship.

What I plan to cite here, however, are nuggets of Jewish wisdom expressing *awareness* of, or *manifestations* of, spirituality in the sense of thinking and feeling—and experiences that elicit thinking and feeling—about the basic mystery behind existence, or obscure hints of the operation of a mind-endowed ground of being.

I begin with the questions which the Book of Job says God uttered with the intention of making Job aware of the great mystery underlying cosmic phenomena ("Where wast thou when I laid the foundations of the earth? ... Whereupon are the foundations thereof fastened? ... Doth the hawk fly by thy wisdom, ... Doth the eagle mount up at thy command ...?").

In the Book of Psalms, we find the suggestion that the heavens and the firmament provide evidences of the existence of a Deity ("The heavens declare the glory of God, and the firmament sheweth his handiwork").

That a spiritually open person should read the Bible for its revelatory symbolical intimations rather than its literal declarations was recommended by Moses Maimonides ("[Biblical] expressions like 'I whet my glittering sword' are metaphorical. Has God a sword? ... It is a figure of speech").

Albert Einstein associated spirituality and religion with an awareness of the great cosmic mystery ("a sense of the mysterious ... is the underlying principle of religion"). He also referred to God as manifesting himself to those who seek basic truth ("My religion consists of a humble admiration of the illimitable superior spirit who reveals himself in the slight details which we are able to perceive with our frail and feeble mind").

Martin Buber reported that a Hasidic master had described any place where one is standing as "holy ground" ("there is no rung of being on which we cannot find the holiness of God").

The elusive but unavoidable Presence of God was described in exquisitely poetic language by the Russian-born American Rabbi Joseph B. Soloveitchik ("Who is He who trails me steadily, ... like an everlasting shadow, and vanishes into ... transcendence the ... instant I turn around to confront this ... mysterious 'He'?").

The Presence of God was also adumbrated by Abraham Joshua Heschel ("Are we alone in the wilderness of time ...? Is there a Presence to live by? ... How embarrassing for man to live in the shadow of greatness ..., to be a contemporary of God and not to sense it!").

Heschel, in addition, associated prayer not with petition but with a sense of spirituality and appreciation of the ubiquity of mystery ("To pray is ... to retain a sense of the mystery that animates all beings. ... Prayer is our humble answer to the ... surprise of living").

Having now tasted examples of the essence of Jewish wisdom as I organized them in five topical categories, you may wish to continue discovering on subsequent pages many eye-opening truths and proposed truths developed by Jewish sages who lived in every period and clime.

Part One

NUGGETS OF WISDOM FROM
JEWISH SCRIPTURAL WRITINGS

I
THE HEBREW BIBLE

In the Jewish perspective, the Bible consists of three basic components, as illustrated in the designation of the Bible, in Jewish lore, by the acronym TANAKH, in which the basic letters have the following meanings:

"T" (with an "a" after it to help in the pronunciation) stands for the Hebrew word "Torah" (that is, the Pentateuch).

"N" (with an "a" after it to help in the pronunciation) stands for the Hebrew word "Nevi'im" (the Prophets).

"K" (with an "h" after it because, in some cases, a "k" at the end of a word becomes "kh") represents "Ketuvim" (the "Writings"; that is, the Psalms, Proverbs, Job, the Song of Songs, etc.).

The nuggets of wisdom appearing on the pages which follow are presented in the order in which the nuggets (and the books containing them) appear in the Bible. But this arrangement does not correspond to the chronology of *composition* of the various extracts (or the books in which they appear).

Although Biblical scholars, both Jewish and non-Jewish, have established, with some exactitude, the chronological order in which priests, prophets, and scribes composed or edited the books of the Bible, I have chosen not to reflect the scholars' findings on this topic, preferring to follow, in my presentation, the sequence (Genesis, Exodus, etc.) with which we are familiar.

1. The Pentateuch

Erudite readers call the first portion of the Bible the Pentateuch (from the Greek word which means "five books"). Jews generally call it the Torah (from the Hebrew word which means "Teaching"). This component of the Bible consists of Genesis, Exodus, Leviticus, Numbers, and Deuteronomy.

A. Genesis

The imaginative description of the creation of the world in the early chapters of Genesis, which captivates us by its word-magic, is now taken literally by only a few readers. Nevertheless, even hard-headed scientists of the present day, and their educated followers, sometimes say—with reference to the beginning of things, as well as the immensely complex uniformities (or "laws") which encompass the world's events—that a divine mind, or at least a Great Conceptual Mystery, may have had something to do with it.

Genesis declares simply, in terms that are open to multiple interpretations:

1   "In the beginning God created the heaven
        and the earth. . . . And God said, Let there be
        light: and there was light."

Curiously, the order in which the next developments reportedly occurred — the appearance of "the dry land Earth," the gathering together of "the Seas," the development of plants and then animals, the arising at last of human beings, and the human achievement of "knowing good and evil" — conforms roughly to the stages outlined in present-day theories of evolution.

The coming of hatred and murder into the world, as exemplified in the story of Cain and Abel, is narrated in Genesis with perceptiveness and insight into the human foundations and meaning of crime and punishment. When Cain was condemned to wander over the earth as "a fugitive and a vagabond," for the sin of fratricide, he commented, according to Scripture:

2   "My punishment is greater than I can bear."

Whereupon, according to the narrative, God mitigated the punishment, assuring Cain that no one, on "finding him, should kill him."

The next impressive nugget in Genesis is found in the story of Abraham's lecture to God on the questionable ethics of severely chastening not only those who are actually guilty of wrongdoing but also their innocent *neighbors*. God, it appears, was considering the complete destruction of Sodom and Gomorrah because, as He said regretfully, "their sin is very grievous."

According to Genesis, Abraham then remarked to God, with reference to the population of Sodom:

3   "Peradventure there be fifty righteous
         within the city: wilt thou also destroy . . . the
         place . . . [despite] the fifty righteous that are
         therein?
             "That be far from thee to do after this man-
         ner, to slay the righteous with the wicked . . .:
         Shall not the Judge of all the earth do right?"

In the ensuing debate with Abraham, God conceded that if there were fifty righteous, or forty-five, or forty, or thirty, or twenty, or even ten, He would refrain from ob-literating the city. Abraham broke off the dialogue before he dared ask God if He would destroy an evil city in which one righteous person dwelt.

B. Exodus

In the course of time, the descendants of Abraham be-came slaves in Egypt. Then, according to the story told in Exodus, Moses—the leader who was to achieve an end to their slavery—was confronted by God from within a burning bush. God instructed Moses regarding the strategy to be followed for achieving the desired libera-tion of Abraham's descendants, who were then desig-nated as the "children of Israel."

At that point, Moses said to God, in effect, When I am asked who sent me on my emancipatory mission, what shall I say? God's reply was in the form of a philosophical assertion concerning His nature or essence. This early formal assertion about what God is has reverberated through the centuries whenever the nature or essence of God has come under serious discussion.

4   "And God said unto Moses, I AM THAT I
         AM: and thus shalt thou say unto the children
         of Israel, I AM has sent me unto you."

Commentators on that passage in Exodus have interpreted the passage to mean: I, God, am the being whose nature or essence it is *to be*. That is, I, God, am a *necessary* being. If I am conceived at all, I must be conceived as *existing*. (This form of talk about God was given a technical name by theologians, who called it "the ontological proof of God's existence.")

After God had redeemed the children of Israel from their bondage in Egypt, they worshipped Him, but the notion of God as the *only* deity did not gain immediate acceptance. For a period, I AM THAT I AM was regarded as the *main* god or the *supreme* god. The notion that He was the supreme god constituted an advance in wisdom over the prevalent paganism which paid homage to a host of supernatural beings of more or less comparable power.

The perception of God as the main deity was expressed by Moses himself (according to Exodus) when, after the children of Israel had safely crossed the Red Sea, Moses sang the following song:

5   "Who is like unto thee, O Lord, among the gods? who is like thee, glorious in holiness, fearful in praises, doing wonders?"

A similar understanding of God as the main god among others appears in the Ten Commandments themselves (chapter 20 of Exodus) in the form of the following injunction:

6   "Thou shalt have no other gods before me."

Some of the additional points made in the Ten Commandments are ethical ideals, as distinguished from religious doctrines. They stipulate, for example, abstention from murdering, robbing, and committing adultery.

Moreover, Moses reportedly received on Mount Sinai not only the Ten Commandments but also a body of supplementary moral guidance. The supplementary precepts included the following:

7   "If thou meet thine enemy's ox or his ass
         going astray, thou shalt surely bring it back to
         him . . . .
              "If thou see the ass of him that hateth thee
         lying under his burden, . . . thou shalt surely
         help with him. . . .
              "Also thou shalt not oppress a stranger."

C. Leviticus

Further ethical precepts given to the children of Israel
during their wanderings after they had left Egypt were
recorded in the Book of Leviticus. Among these precepts
are the following:

8   "Thou shalt not defraud thy neighbor . . .:
         the wages of him that is hired shall not abide
         with thee all night until the morning.
              "Thou shalt not . . . put a stumbling block
         before the blind . . . .
              "[T]hou shalt love thy neighbour as thy-
         self . . . .
              "Thou shalt rise up before the hoary head,
         and honour the face of an old man . . . .
              "And   if   thy   brother   be   waxen
         poor, . . . then shalt thou relieve him: yea,
         though he be a stranger . . . . "

D. Numbers

In connection with the taking of a census of the children of Israel, which is the theme of the Book of Numbers, still other moral doctrines were stated, including
the idea that if you embezzle a sum of money, you shall
not only repay that specific amount, but also convey an
additional twenty percent to serve as compensation for
pain:

9   "When   a   man . . . shall   commit   any
         sin . . . he shall recompense his trespass with
         the principal thereof, and add unto it the fifth
         part thereof, and give it unto him against
         whom he hath trespassed."

The Book of Numbers also includes the text of a personal blessing by one person of another which is one of the most moving expressions of good will and beneficence in all of the world's scriptural literature:

10   "The Lord bless thee, and keep thee:
        "The Lord make his face shine upon thee,
        and be gracious unto thee:
        "The Lord lift up his countenance upon thee,
        and give thee peace."

In addition, praise of the virtue of humility appears in the following passage in the Book of Numbers:

11   "Now the man Moses was very meek, above
        all the men which were upon the face of the
        earth."

E. Deuteronomy

Deuteronomy is the only book in the Bible about which the Bible itself tells of the book's coming to light. According to the Second Book of Kings, Deuteronomy was "discovered" in the Temple in Jerusalem by the High Priest in the year of the reign of King Josiah corresponding, in the present calendar, to the year 622 B.C.E. (Before the Common Era). Some scholars hold that the High Priest wrote the book and "planted" it where it could be discovered, but this hypothesis is not universally accepted.

In one of Moses' farewell sermons to the children of Israel, as recorded in Deuteronomy, the belief (mentioned above) that God is the supreme god yet not the only one was emphatically rejected. Instead, according to Moses, not only is God supreme, but *there is no other*. Moses introduced his mature thinking on this subject with these words:

12   "Now these are the commandments, the
        statutes, and the judgments, which the Lord
        your God commanded to teach you, that ye
        might do them in the land whither ye go to possess it."

Then Moses proclaimed:

13   "Hear, O Israel: the Lord our God, the Lord
      is one."

The verse just quoted is taken from the English translation of the Bible published by the Jewish Publication Society of America. I have used that translation for this
verse because, although all other extracts from the Hebrew Bible in the present volume are quoted from the
King James version, this particular verse as rendered by
the King James committee is ambiguous.

The King James version of the verse reads: "Hear, O
Israel: the Lord our God is one Lord." But if He is *one*
Lord, does that mean that there are others? Not according to the original Hebrew text, which says, in the closing
part of the verse, "the Lord is *one*"; that is to say: the Lord
alone is God; He does not share his divinity with others;
He is *uniquely* God.

The "Hear, O Israel" verse has become an epitomiza-
tion of the Jewish credo. Typically, a Jew pronounces
that verse when death is imminent—in martyrdom or
otherwise.

In the same sermon, as it appears in Deuteronomy,
Moses issued these imperatives:

14   "And thou shalt love the Lord thy God with
      all thine heart, and with all thy soul, and with
      all thy might.
         "And these words, which I command thee
      this day, shall be in thine heart:
         "And thou shalt teach them diligently unto
      thy children, and shalt talk of them when thou
      sittest in thy house, and when thou walkest by
      the way, and when thou liest down, and when
      thou risest up."

2. The Prophets

The second segment of the Bible, which is called "The
Prophets," includes not only the writings of the paradig-
matic prophets (such as Isaiah and Micah) but also several historical works (First and Second Books of Samuel,
First and Second Books of Kings, etc.).

In my selections of wisdom literature from the Pentateuch, I found in each of the five books manifestations of wisdom which were eminently worthy of inclusion in the present anthology. In the case of "The Prophets," however, some of the books will be skipped over, because I wish to hold out to my readers only the peak instances of illuminating observations on the world and life.

After the death of Moses, the children of Israel entered the promised land of Canaan and dwelt there. Administrative decisions relating to their public lives were made originally by leaders called judges and, later, by a series of kings, some of whom reigned admirably while others did not.

In the course of time, a category of moral and spiritual guides arose in the promised land whom we now call prophets. The sequence of prophetic books in the Bible (which we shall follow here) does not, however, correspond to the prophets' sermonizing. Readers who wish to locate the prophets' nuggets of wisdom in the ongoing flow of time may find useful the accompanying outline of the geographical and chronological milieu of the prophets who will be quoted.

A. Second Book of Samuel

A story which illustrates the notion that a king, when he acts wrongly, may be chastised by a respected member of the community, is that of King David (tenth century B.C.E.) and the prophet Nathan. King David not only had taken as a mistress the wife of one of his soldiers but had contrived to have the soldier struck down in battle.

The prophet Nathan confronted King David with a report that a wayfarer in the land had selfishly appropriated the beloved lamb of a poor farmer. Without hesitation, the king decreed that the wayfarer should be punished. At that point, Nathan dramatically announced:

Context of the Prophets' Preaching, B.C.E

I. The "United Kingdom"
   (Kings Saul, David, and Solomon)

Tenth century . . . . NATHAN

II. Breakup into Israel and Judah

	Israel (north)	Judah (south, including Jerusalem)
Ninth century . . .	ELIJAH	
Eighth century . . .	HOSEA	ISAIAH
	AMOS	MICAH

(Israel disappears after conquest by Assyria)

Seventh century . . . . DEUTERO-HOSEA
Sixth century . . . . MALACHI

---

15   "Thou art the man. . . .
        "Wherefore hast thou despised the com-
mandment of the Lord, to do evil in his sight?"

B. First Book of Kings

The wisdom of the prophet Elijah, as recorded in the First Book of Kings, will occupy us next.

One of the prophet Elijah's contributions was the idea—conveyed to his compatriots in the northern kingdom of Israel—that God may properly be symbolized not as resembling an earthquake or a raging fire but as a still small voice. Elijah reported an encounter with God—an epiphany—in the following expressive words:

16   "[A] great and strong wind rent the moun-
        tains, . . . but the Lord was not in the wind:
        "[A]nd after the wind an earthquake; but the
        Lord was not in the earthquake:
        "And after the earthquake a fire; but the
        Lord was not in the fire:
        "[A]nd after the fire a still small voice."

C. First Book of Chronicles

From the First Book of Chronicles, I wish to quote a nugget of wisdom which is ascribed in that book to King David. Having assembled "all the princes of Israel, the princes of the tribes, and the captains," David in their presence expressed his reverence toward the Almighty, as follows:

17   "Thine, O Lord, is the greatness and the power and the glory and the victory and the majesty; for all that is in the heaven and in the earth is thine; thine is the kingdom, O Lord, and thou art exalted as head above all."

D. Isaiah

The next important prophetic book in the Bible is ascribed to Isaiah. According to scholars, however, only the first thirty-nine chapters of the book were written by the eighth-century prophet himself (Isaiah ben Amoz), while chapters 40 to 66 were written by an unknown preacher (Deutero-Isaiah; that is, Second Isaiah), probably during the sixth century.

In chapter 1, Isaiah eloquently extolled moral rectitude in language which has often been quoted.

18   "Wash you, make you clean; put away the evil of your doings before mine eyes; . . . .
       "Learn to do well; . . . relieve the oppressed, judge the fatherless, plead for the widow."

He explained to his hearers that there was still time to undertake a new way of living:

19   "Come now, and let us reason together, saith the Lord: though your sins be as scarlet, they shall be as white as snow; though they be red like crimson, they shall be as wool."

In chapter 2, Isaiah predicted a future era of social tranquility and peace:

20   "[O]ut of Zion shall go forth the law, and the
        word of the Lord from Jerusalem.
        "[A]nd they shall beat their swords into
        ploughshares, and their spears into pruning-
        hooks; nation shall not lift up sword against
        nation, neither shall they learn war any more."

Isaiah's prediction about the beating of swords into
ploughshares was quoted by U.S. President Jimmy Car-
ter (a Christian), Israeli Prime Minister Menachem Begin
(a Jew), and Egyptian President Anwar Sadat (a Moslem)
on the White House lawn in 1978, when announcing the
peace agreement between Israel and Egypt.

(The two verses just quoted from Isaiah also appear,
with almost the exact wording, in the book of Micah. The
prophet Micah was a contemporary of Isaiah, who
preached, along with Isaiah, in the southern kingdom of
Judah.)

In chapter 5, Isaiah portrayed as follows the disap-
pointment of the Lord with the moral backsliding of the
residents of Judah:

21   "[H]e looked for judgment, but behold op-
        pression, for righteousness, but behold a cry."

Isaiah continued with a denunciation of drunken dissi-
pation and the overturning of standards:

22   "Woe unto them that rise up early in the
        morning, that they may follow strong drink;
        that continue until night, till wine inflame
        them! . . .
        "Woe unto them that call evil good, and
        good evil; that put darkness for light, and light
        for darkness."

In chapter 6, Isaiah recounted a mystical vision which
has resonated in many efforts of the pious to think about
heaven.

23   "I saw . . . the Lord sitting upon a throne,
        high and lifted up, and his train filled the tem-
        ple.

"Above it stood the seraphims: each one had
six wings; with twain he covered his face, and
with twain he covered his feet, and with twain
he did fly.
"And one cried to another, and said, Holy,
holy, holy, is the Lord of hosts; the whole earth
is full of his glory."

Isaiah also narrated how he had volunteered for service in restoring lofty standards.

24   "Also I heard the voice of the Lord, saying,
Whom shall I send, and who will go for us?
Then said I, Here am I; send me."

This is an echo of the call and the response narrated in
the First Book of Samuel (chapter 3, verse 4), namely,
"[T]he Lord called Samuel: and he answered, Here am I."

In chapter 7, Isaiah made a prediction about the birth
of a son to be called Immanuel ("With Us Is God"). This
prediction, along with Isaiah's words in chapter 9
(quoted below), is interpreted by some Christians as a
reference to Jesus about seven hundred years before his
birth.

25   "Behold, a virgin shall conceive, and bear a
son, and shall call his name Immanuel."

Jewish commentators point out (a) that the word
which the King James committee translated as "a virgin"
more probably means a young girl, and (b) that Isaiah
was encouraging the then-king of Judah, Ahaz, to believe that certain neighboring attackers against Judah
would fail.

In chapter 9, we find a further cryptic utterance regarding a remarkable child.

26   "For unto us a child is born, unto us a son is
given; and the government shall be upon his
shoulder: and his name shall be called Won-
derful, Counsellor, the mighty God, the Everlasting Father, the Prince of Peace."

(Jewish translators, using a text based on newly available ancient manuscripts, have come out with different language, such as "The mighty God is planning grace, the Puissant One of Jacob intends peace." The words of the King James free translation, however, were used with striking effect by the composer Handel in his oratorio "The Messiah.")

A further prediction occurs in chapter 11 of Isaiah, about an end to strife.

27   "The wolf . . . shall dwell with the lamb, and the leopard shall lie down with the kid; . . . and a little child shall lead them. . . .
"They shall not hurt nor destroy in all my holy mountain."

(A variant of what is said in these two verses appears in Deutero-Isaiah's chapter 65, verse 25.)

My last extract from the preachings of the original Isaiah (that is, chapters 1-30) foretells a better day for educators.

28   "[T]hough the Lord give you the bread of adversity and the water of affliction, yet shall not thy teachers be removed into a corner any more."

Deutero-Isaiah was as fond of wisdom-infused predictions as the original Isaiah was. In chapter 35, Deutero-Isaiah foretold a time of prosperity and joy.

29   "[T]he desert shall rejoice, and blossom as the rose. . . .
"And the ransomed of the Lord shall return, and come to Zion with songs and everlasting joy upon their heads; . . . sorrow and sighing shall flee away."

Chapter 40 of Deutero-Isaiah contains a further delineation of an amelioration of trouble.

30   "Comfort ye, comfort ye my people, saith your God.
"Speak ye comfortably to Jerusalem, and cry

unto her, that her warfare is accomplished,
that her iniquity is pardoned: . . . .
 "Every valley shall be exalted, and every
mountain and hill shall be made low: and the
crooked shall be made straight, and the rough
places plain."

This resounding passage also was used by Handel in
"The Messiah."

In chapter 58, Deutero-Isaiah contrasted a purely ritual
fast with a fast which entails helping the under-
privileged.

31   "[Y]e shall not fast as ye do this day, to make
your voice to be heard on high.
 "Is it such a fast that I have chosen? . . . .
[I]s it . . . to spread sackcloth and ashes . . . ?
 "Is not *this* the fast I have chosen? to loose
the bands of wickedness, to undo the heavy
burdens, to let the oppressed go free, and that
ye break every yoke?
 "Is it not to deal thy bread to the hungry,
. . . when thou seest the naked, that thou
cover him . . . ?"

E. Jeremiah

After Isaiah's book comes the Book of Jeremiah. The
prophet Jeremiah lived in the period when the Babylonian Empire conquered the kingdom of Judah and exiled
its inhabitants to the city of Babylon for fifty years (587 to
about 537 B.C.E.).

In chapter 6 of his book, Jeremiah lamented the fact
that, although people generally praised peace, there was
no peace.

32   "They have healed . . . the hurt of the
daughter of my people *slightly*, saying, Peace,
peace; when there is no peace."

(This text is repeated in chapter 8, verse 11, of
Jeremiah, and a variant of it is found in Ezekiel, chapter
13, verse 10.)

In another part of chapter 8, Jeremiah noted the sad circumstances of his people, and he asked:

33   "Is there no balm in Gilead; is there no physician there?"

In chapter 17, Jeremiah advocated faith in an ultimate return of the nation to a peaceful mode of existence.

34   "Blessed is the man that trusteth in the Lord,
        and whose hope the Lord is.
        "For he shall be as a tree planted by the waters, and that spreadeth out her roots by the river."

Another promising oracle was voiced by Jeremiah in his chapter 33.

35   "Again there shall be heard in this place . . .
        "The voice of joy, and the voice of the gladness, the voice of the bridegroom, and the voice of the bride, the voice of them that say, . . . the Lord is good; for his mercy endureth for ever."

F. Hosea

Several prophetic books follow at this point in the Bible, which are by no means arranged in the chronological order of their composition. The chronological order, however, is complicated, some of the books having been written and later edited over a range of a few centuries.

The Book of Hosea was apparently composed by the prophet Hosea (eighth century B.C.E.) in the kingdom of *Israel*, but was revised, after the fall of Israel, in *Judah*. The book as we now have it consists of chapters 1-3 (probably written by Hosea) and chapters 4-14 (probably written by Deutero-Hosea).

Deutero-Hosea wrote in chapter 7 about the unhappy consequences of evildoing.

36   "[T]hey have sown the wind, and they shall reap the whirlwind."

G. Amos

Hosea's book is followed by that of Amos, who preached in the northern state of Israel in the eighth century. One of Amos's messages is similar to (but preceded) Deutero-Isaiah's already quoted admonition to the southern kingdom of Judah in the sixth century; namely, that feeding the hungry and clothing the naked are more acceptable to God than ritual fasting. Amos's similar guidance on this topic took the form of a pronouncement ascribed by Amos to Almighty God.

37   "Though ye offer me burnt offerings . . . ,
       I will not accept them . . . .
          "But let judgment run down as waters, and
       righteousness as a mighty stream."

H. Micah

Micah (eighth century, Judah) made a highly significant point by asking:

38   "[W]hat doth the Lord require of thee, but to
       do justly, and to love mercy, and to walk hum-
       bly with thy God?"

I. Malachi

Malachi is the last of the prophets whose uplifting wisdom I shall here purvey. From the fact that the word "Malachi" means "my messenger," together with the appearance (near the beginning of the Book of Malachi) of the words "Behold, I will send my messenger," scholars have inferred that Malachi is a *designation* rather than a personal name; in other words, the book is anonymous.

Written in Judah after the return from exile in Babylon, the book contains a metaphorical verse which reflects a well-known Egyptian religious aphorism.

39   "[U]nto you that fear my name shall the Sun
       of righteousness arise with healing in his
       wings."

3. The "Writings"

The third and last segment of the Hebrew Bible is "Ketuvim" (Writings). Some scholars call this segment "Hagiographa" (which is Greek for "Holy Writings"). It consists of:

> Six books which are primarily literary (Job, Psalms, Proverbs, Ecclesiastes, Song of Songs, and Lamentations) and
> Seven books which are primarily historical (Ruth, First and Second Books of Chronicles, Ezra, Nehemiah, Esther, and Daniel).

Of this total of thirteen books, we shall quote selected passages from six, taken in the order in which they appear in the Bible (Ruth from the above list of historical works, and the first five from the above list of literary works).

A. Ruth

The Book of Ruth was probably written in the time of the united kingdom (tenth century B.C.E.). It begins with the statement that, "in the days when the judges ruled" (that is, in the fourteenth century B.C.E.), Elimelech was a Hebrew sojourner in the nearby land of Moab, with his wife Naomi and their two sons. The story proceeds with an account of the death of Elimelech and his two sons, both of whom had married Moabite women.

The widow Naomi then sets out to return to her native Canaan, the home of her fellow Israelites. Of her two Moabite daughters-in-law, one—Ruth—insisted on returning with her, despite Naomi's efforts to dissuade her.

Ruth's eloquent expression of resolve to accompany her mother-in-law to the land of the Israelites is a classic formula of determination to pursue a chosen path.

40   "Intreat me not to leave thee, or to return
       from following after thee: for whither thou
       goest, I will go; and where thou lodgest, I will

lodge: thy people shall be my people, and thy
God my God.

"Where thou diest, will I die, and there will I
be buried: the Lord do so to me [pretending by
a gesture to slit her own throat], and more also,
if ought but death part thee and me."

Ruth, in the story, becomes an ancestor of the lovingly
admired King David.

B. Book of Job

The Book of Job, another scroll in the Ketuvim, nar-
rates the tribulations of a man who "feared God, and es-
chewed evil," and whose faith was tried by a series of
catastrophes. Early in the book, Job proclaimed:

41   "Naked came I out of my mother's womb,
        and naked shall I return thither: the Lord gave,
        and the Lord hath taken away; blessed be the
        name of the Lord."

As to the idea of returning "thither," perhaps the reference is to Mother Nature, from which all of us came and
to which we shall all return.

Although Job seemed to say in the above-quoted verse
that he accepted philosophically the adversities to which
he had been subjected, at another place in the book he
takes a different stance, saying that it would have been
better had he not been born, and that the dead are at least
at rest. On the first of these two points, he said:

42   "Why died I not from the womb? Why did I
        not give up the ghost when I came out of the
        belly?"

On the second point, he spoke as follows:

43   "There [among the dead] the wicked cease
        from troubling; and there the weary be at rest.
            "There the prisoners . . . hear not the voice
        of the oppressor . . . and the servant is free
        from his master."

Of the friends who sought to comfort Job, or to convince him that his suffering was due to his sins, one (Eliphaz, from Yemen) asserted the following as an aphorism:

44   "[M]an is born unto trouble, as the sparks fly
       upward."

The same friend also remarked that God sometimes afflicts a person but later makes amends:

45   "[H]e maketh sore, and bindeth up: he
       woundeth, and his hands make whole."

Job, having heard the learned comments of his friends regarding his unhappy situation, gave his own analysis of the human condition in two trenchant propositions, namely, first, technical skill can enable us to transform the face of nature, but, secondly, we nevertheless are vastly deficient in wisdom. He said:

46   "[M]an overturneth . . . mountains . . . .
       "He bindeth the floods from overflowing;
       and the thing that is hid bringeth he forth to
       light.
       "But where shall wisdom be found? and
       where is the place of understanding?
       "Man knoweth not the price thereof . . . ."

In addition, on a narrower aspect of human life (the critical reception that awaits wielders of the pen), Job said, in a cynical tone:

47   "[B]ehold, my desire is, that . . . mine ad-
       versary had written a book."

Finally, we learn what seems to be the lesson taught us by the story of Job. That lesson, I think, is that neither Job nor any other human being is able to fathom God's infinite scope or the strategy of the cosmic plan. The lesson is expressed in two speeches, containing some of the most elegant poetic expressions not only in the whole Bible but in all of world literature.

— In the first speech, Job's neighbor Elihu says to Job,

in effect, Who do you think you are in trying to second-guess God?

— In the second speech, God conveys the same message: Who do you think you are in trying to second-guess me?

Elihu's speech reads in part:

48   "[God] saith to the snow, Be thou on the earth; likewise to the small rain, and to the great rain of his strength. . . .

"Dost thou know . . . the wondrous works of him which is perfect in knowledge? . . . .

"Hast thou with him spread out the sky . . . ?

"Touching the Almighty, we cannot find him out: he is excellent in power, and in judgment."

This put-down is followed by the shattering finale, God discoursing to Job (introduced by the fateful words "Then the Lord answered Job out of the whirlwind"):

49   "Who is this that darkeneth counsel by words without knowledge?

"Gird up now thy loins . . . ; for I will demand of thee, and answer thou me.

"Where wast thou when I laid the foundations of the earth? declare, if thou hast understanding.

"Who hath laid the measures thereof, if thou knowest? . . . .

"Whereupon are the foundations thereof fastened? or who laid the corner stone thereof;

"When the morning stars sang together . . . ?

"Or who shut up the sea with doors, when it brake forth, . . .?

"Hast thou commanded the morning since thy days; and caused the dayspring to know his place . . .?

"Where is the way where light dwelleth? and

as for darkness, where is the place
thereof . . .?

"Hast thou entered into the treasures of the
snow? or hast thou seen the treasures of the
hail . . .?

"Hath the rain a father? or who hath begot-
ten the drops of dew? . . . .

"Knowest thou the ordinances of heaven?
Canst thou set the dominion thereof in the
earth? . . . .

"Who hath put wisdom in the inward parts?
or who hath given understanding to the
heart? . . . .

"Doth the hawk fly by thy wisdom, and
stretch her wings toward the south?

"Doth the eagle mount up at thy command,
and make her nest on high?"

C. Psalms

Immediately following the starkly dramatic Book of
Job, in the Biblical canon, is another book of paramount
religious importance, the Book of Psalms. Many of the
compositions in the Book of Psalms are of unparalleled
literary and spiritual exquisiteness. They are, furthermore, sprinkled with nuggets of deep religious fervor
and general wisdom.

The Book of Psalms is divided into five parts (Psalms 1-
41, 42-72, 73-89, 90-106, and 107-150), each of which—
except the fifth—ends with a short colophon, marking
the end of a major segment. For example, Psalm 72 (end
of the second section) concludes as follows:

— Verse 18, "Blessed be the Lord God, the God of Israel, who only doeth wondrous things."

— Verse 19, "And blessed be his glorious name for
ever: and let the whole earth be filled with his glory;
Amen, and Amen."

— Verse 20, "The prayers of David the son of Jesse are
ended."

On the basis of the foregoing considerations and other pertinent data, students of the Bible have concluded that the Book of Psalms is an edited compilation, rather than the work of a single auther. It is true that many of the psalms are headed, in the Hebrew text, "le-David"; that is, *of* David or *about* (or with reference to) David, a fact which led to the tradition that David the soulful king wrote the psalms. That tradition, however, does not stand up in the light of meticulous linguistic and historical analysis.

Striking passages in the psalms often reflect a conception of God and His relations with human beings which differs in important particulars from prevalent theological thinking in our day. Nevertheless, I shall call some of those passages nuggets of wisdom because of their imaginative splendor and the fact that they may be taken as metaphorical expressions of credible beliefs.

Nuggets in the First Section (Psalms 1-41). We begin with two challenging verses in Psalm 1.

50   "Blessed is the man that walketh not in the counsel of the ungodly, nor standeth in the way of sinners, nor sitteth in the seat of the scornful.

"But his delight is in the law of the Lord; and in his law doth he meditate day and night."

Psalm 8 turns to the topic of the interrelationship that prevails between God and human beings.

51   "When I consider thy heavens, the work of thy fingers, the moon and the stars, which thou hast ordained;

"What is man, that thou art mindful of him? and the son of man, that thou visitest him?

"For thou hast made him a little lower than the angels, and hast crowned him with glory and honour. . . .

"O Lord our Lord, how excellent is thy name in all the earth!"

Psalm 15, in the manner of Psalm 1; stresses the blessed state of those who are of upright heart.

52   "Lord, who shall abide in thy tabernacle? who shall dwell in thy holy hill?

"He that walketh uprightly, and worketh righteousness, and speaketh the truth in his heart."

In Psalm 19, we read of God's glory.

53   "The heavens declare the glory of God; and the firmament sheweth his handiwork. . . .

"The law of the Lord is perfect, converting the soul: the testimony of the Lord is sure, making wise the simple.

"The statutes of the Lord are right, rejoicing the heart: the commandment of the Lord is pure, enlightening the eyes.

"The fear of the Lord is clean, enduring for ever: the judgments of the Lord are true and righteous altogether. . . .

"Let the words of my mouth, and the meditation of my heart, be acceptable in thy sight, O Lord, my strength, and my redeemer."

As to the next selection in this garland from part 1, many people know it by heart. It is the solacing Twenty-third Psalm.

54   "The Lord is my shepherd; I shall not want.

"He maketh me to lie down in green pastures; he leadeth me beside the still waters.

"He restoreth my soul: he leadeth me in the paths of righteousness for his name's sake.

"Yea, though I walk through the valley of the shadow of death, I will fear no evil: for thou art with me; thy rod and thy staff they comfort me.

"Thou preparest a table before me in the presence of mine enemies: thou anointest my head with oil; my cup runneth over.

"Surely goodness and mercy shall follow me

all the days of my life: and I will dwell in the
house of the Lord for ever."

Almost as touching as the Twenty-third Psalm are
parts of the Twenty-fourth.

55   "The earth is the Lord's, and the fullness
        thereof; the world, and they that dwell therein.
           "For he hath founded it upon the seas, and
        established it upon the floods.
           "Who shall ascend into the hill of the Lord?
        or who shall stand in his holy place?
           "He that hath clean hands, and a pure heart;
        who hath not lifted up his soul unto vanity, nor
        sworn deceitfully."

Nuggets in the Third Section (Psalms 73 to 89). Skipping the second section (Psalms 42-72), I shall now present a wisdom utterance from the group formed by numbers 73 to 89.

Psalm 84 graphically portrays the difference between
piety and impiety.

56   "I had rather be a doorkeeper in the house of
        my God, than to dwell in the tents of wicked-
        ness."

Nuggets in the Fourth Section (Psalms 90 to 106).
Psalm 90 points out how time is viewed from the
standpoint of an eternal mind.

57   "[A] thousand years in thy sight are but as
        yesterday when it is past, and as a watch in the
        night."

Psalm 92 extols songs of praise to the Almighty.

58   "It is a good thing to give thanks unto the
        Lord, and to sing praises unto thy name, O
        most High:
           "To shew forth thy lovingkindness in the
        morning, and thy faithfulness every night,
           "Upon an instrument of ten strings, and

upon the psaltery; upon the harp with a solemn sound."

Nuggets in the Fifth Section (Psalms 107-150). Psalm 107 reminds us of the control of the Eternal Mind over the weather.

59   "They that go down to the sea in ships, that do business in great waters;

"These see the works of the Lord, and his wonders in the deep.

"For he commandeth, and raiseth the stormy wind, which lifteth up the waves thereof. . . .

"[T]hey cry unto the Lord in their trouble, and he bringeth them out of their distresses.

"He maketh the storm to calm, so that the waves thereof are still. . . .

"[S]o he bringeth them unto their desired haven."

Psalm 136 consists of twenty-six verses, most of which consist of (a) a few words describing a ground for giving thanks to the Lord, and (b) the formula "for his mercy endureth for ever." I shall quote the first part of selected verses, but I shall include the words "for his mercy endureth for ever" at the end of only the first and last of the selected verses.

60   "To him that by wisdom made the heavens: for his mercy endureth for ever.

"To him that stretched out the earth above the waters: . . . .

"To him that made great lights: . . . .

"The sun to rule by day: . . . .

"The moon and stars to rule by night: . . . .

"O give thanks unto the God of heaven: for his mercy endureth for ever."

D. Proverbs

The Book of Psalms, from which the foregoing nuggets were extracted, is immediately followed, in the pages of the Bible, by the Book of Proverbs. Who wrote the Book of Proverbs? The text itself contains the following indications:

— Chapter 1 begins "The proverbs of Solomon the son of David king of Israel."

— Chapter 10 begins "The proverbs of Solomon."

— Chapter 25 begins "These are also proverbs of Solomon, which the men of Hezekiah king of Judah copied out."

— Chapter 30 begins "The words of Agur the son of Jakeh, even the prophecy: the man spake unto Ithiel, even unto Ithiel and Ucal."

— Chapter 31 begins "The words of king Lemuel, the prophecy that his mother taught him."

Other pertinent facts include the following:

— Parts of chapters 22-24 contain thirty precepts closely resembling the Egyptian wisdom book entitled "Instruction of Amen-em-ope."

— Chapter 24, verse 23, seems to be a heading of a separate collection of unascribed (perhaps anonymous) proverbs. It begins "These things also belong to the wise."

Bible scholars, in summary, are agreed that the Book of Proverbs contains material originating in periods ranging from the tenth century (Solomonic period) to the first century B.C.E.

The book includes not only substantive words of wisdom but also, in chapter 3, noteworthy words *in praise of wisdom*, with which we now begin our group of nuggets.

61   "Happy is the man that findeth wisdom, and
        the man that getteth understanding.
             "For the merchandise of it is better than the
        merchandise of silver, and the gain thereof
        than fine gold.
             "She is more precious than rubies: and all the

things thou canst desire are not to be compared to her.

"Length of days is in her right hand; and in her left hand riches and honour.

"Her ways are ways of pleasantness, and all her paths are peace.

"She is a tree of life to them that lay hold upon her: and happy is every one that retaineth her."

Chapter 6 chides those who are lazy.

62   "Go to the ant, thou sluggard, consider her ways, and be wise.

"Which having no guide, overseer, or ruler,

"Provideth her meat in the summer, and gathereth her food in the harvest."

A litany of forms of depravity appears later in the same chapter.

63   "These six things doth the Lord hate: yea, seven are an abomination unto him.

"A proud look, a lying tongue, and hands that shed innocent blood,

"A heart that deviseth wicked imaginations, feet that be swift in running to mischief,

"A false witness that speaketh lies, and he that soweth discord among brethren."

A further eulogy to wisdom, as having existed before the creation of the world (a Platonic eternal archetype?), is an ornament of chapter 8.

64   "The Lord possessed me in the beginning of his way, before his works of old.

"I was set up from everlasting, from the beginning, or ever the earth was. . . .

"When he prepared the heavens, I was there: when he set a compass upon the face of the depth: . . . .

"Now therefore hearken unto me, O ye children: for blessed are they that keep my ways.

"Hear instruction, and be wise."

Chapter 15 commends patience and family love.

65   "A soft answer turneth away wrath: but
        grievous words stir up anger. . . .
        "Better is a dinner of herbs where love is,
        than a stalled ox and hatred therewith."

Chapter 16 also extols patience.

66   "He that is slow to anger is better than the
        mighty; and he that ruleth his spirit than he
        that taketh a city."

Wisdom in the field of value education is the topic of a consummately expressed verse in chapter 22.

67   "Train up a child in the way he should go:
        and when he is old, he will not depart from it."

The uncertainty of the future is the wisdom of a verse in chapter 27.

68   "Boast not thyself of to morrow; for thou
        knowest not what a day may bring forth."

Chapter 30 affirms that even in the case of everyday things there is an unending mystery.

69   "There be three things which are too won-
        derful for me, yea, four which I know not:
        "The way of an eagle in the air; the way of a
        serpent upon a rock; the way of a ship in the
        midst of the sea; and the way of a man with a
        maid."

The Book of Proverbs ends with resounding praise of an upright woman. The paean is an acrostic, in which the first letter of each line begins with a letter of the Hebrew alphabet, from *alef* at the beginning to *tav* at the end.

70   "Who can find a virtuous woman? for her
        price is far above rubies.
        "The heart of her husband doth safely trust
        in her . . . .
        "She will do him good and not evil all the
        days of her life. . . .

"She stretcheth out her hands to the poor;
yea, she reacheth forth her hands to the needy.
. . .

"Strength and honour are her clothing;
. . . .

"She openeth her mouth with wisdom: and
in her tongue is the law of kindness. . . .
"Her children arise up, and call her blessed;
her husband also, and he praiseth her."

E. Ecclesiastes

After Proverbs, the next component of the "Writings"
in the Bible is the Book of Ecclesiastes, which—like
Proverbs—is rich in wisdom pronouncements. In the
Hebrew text, the opening words of Ecclesiastes (in-
tended as the by-line) are *Dibrei Kohelet* (Words of
Kohelet), and the author is identified as "the son of
David, king of Jerusalem"; that is, Solomon.

Facts bearing on the actual authorship of the book, as
unearthed by scholars, include the following:

— The book was originally written not in Hebrew but
in Aramaic, and the name of the author in the Aramaic
original was Kahla (which can mean either "Female Convoker" or "*The* Convoker," probably intended as the latter in this case).

— Kahla became Kohelet (Female Convoker) when the
book was translated into Hebrew, Ecclesiastes (Convoker) in the Septuagint translation of the Bible into
Greek, and the Preacher in the King James translation.

— The vocabulary and idioms used in the book indicate that the period of its composition was several centuries after Solomon's lifetime.

I now turn to nuggets which may be dug up from the
Book of Ecclesiastes.

Chapter 1 of the book reflects a mood of disillusion
without depression.

71   "Vanity of vanities, saith the Preacher, van-
        ity of vanities; all is vanity.

"What profit hath a man of all his labour
which he taketh under the sun?

"One generation passeth away, and another
generation cometh: but the earth abideth for
ever. . . .

"All rivers run into the sea; yet the sea is not
full; unto the place from whence the rivers
come, thither they return again. . . .

"The thing that hath been, it is that which
shall be; . . . and there is no new thing under
the sun. . . .

"I gave my heart to know wisdom, and to
know madness and folly: I perceived that this
also is vexation of spirit.

"For in much wisdom is much grief: and he
that increaseth knowledge increaseth sorrow."

The author wrote in a more positive vein, and with
greater practical utility, in chapter 3.

72   "To every thing there is a season, and a time
to every purpose under the heaven:

"A time to be born, and a time to die; a time
to plant, and a time to pluck up that which is
planted; . . .

"A time to weep, and a time to laugh; a time
to mourn, and a time to dance; . . .

"A time to get, and a time to lose; a time to
keep, and a time to cast away;

" . . . [A] time to keep silence, and a time to
speak;

"A time to love, and a time to hate."

F. Song of Songs

We come now to the last of the Biblical "Writings" from
which illuminating aphorisms or oracles will be quoted
in this collection of nuggets of wisdom. The Song of
Songs, with authorship assigned to King Solomon in its
opening words, is an erotic conversation between a man
and a woman, with not a single reference to God or religion in the whole book.

The inclusion of the book in the official Hebrew Bible was vigorously disputed until the year 90 B.C.E., when a council of rabbis, at Yavneh (in Palestine), accepted the plea of the famous Rabbi Akivah that the book should be included—as an allegory standing for the mutual love of God and the people of Israel. Akivah argued:

> "[A]ll the Writings are holy, but the Song of Songs is the Holy of Holies."

In Christianity, allegorists describe the Song of Songs as referring to the mutual love of Jesus and the church.

The literal interpretation of the book, as a series of love songs, was recently given a religious tinge by Professor Keith N. Scoville, of the University of Wisconsin, who said:

> "The redeeming value of this view [the literal interpretation], if one is needed, is that love in all its manifestations is the work of the Creator who made all things and pronounced them good."

The period of composition of the book, or of its parts, is assigned by experts to the period between 800 and 400 B.C.E. Excerpts from the Song of Songs are reproduced here as representing a philosophy of celebration of physical love.

a. Near the beginning of the conversation, the woman says:

73   "A bundle of myrrh is my well-beloved unto me; he shall lie all night betwixt my breasts.
        . . .

        "I am the rose of Sharon, and the lily of the valleys. . . .
        "The voice of my beloved! behold, he cometh leaping upon the mountains, skipping upon the hills."

b. The man then takes up the conversation.

74   "Behold, thou art fair, my love; behold, thou art fair: . . . .

"Thy lips are like a thread of scarlet, and thy speech is comely . . . .

"Thy two breasts are like two young roes that are twins . . . .

"Thou hast ravished my heart, my sister, my spouse: . . . .

"[H]ow much better is thy love than wine! and the smell of thine ointments than all spices! . . .

"[H]oney and milk are under thy tongue . . . ."

c. Then the woman speaks again.

75   "My beloved is . . . ruddy, the chiefest among ten thousand.

"His head is as the most fine gold, ...

"His belly is as bright ivory overlaid with sapphires. . . .

"His mouth is most sweet; yea, he is altogether lovely."

d. Then it is the man's turn.

76   "How beautiful are thy feet with shoes, O prince's daughter! the joints of thy thighs are like jewels, . . .

"Thy navel is like a round goblet, ...

"How fair and how pleasant art thou, O love, for delights!

". . . [T]hy stature is like to a palm tree, and thy breasts to clusters of grapes."

II
THE DEAD SEA SCROLLS

Ancient manuscripts of unprecedented value were found in 1947 and succeeding years in and near the settlement of Khirbat Qumran on the northwest shore of the Dead Sea. Among these manuscripts was one, entitled *Serekh ha-Yakhad* (Manual of Discipline), which summarized the outlook of a Jewish ascetic sect that dwelt in that area around 100 B.C.E.

The members of the sect—male voluntary celibates—believed in an early "end of days," when righteousness would triumph over evil. They lived communally, eating together and pooling their possessions, and subjected candidates for admission to the group to periods of trial membership. Many scholars, though not all, identify the sect with the Essenes, a Jewish group known from other sources to have followed ascetic practices.

The Manual of Discipline which was found with the other manuscripts contains a goodly number of discerning pronouncements, a selection of which will be presented here.

Section 1 of the Manual specifies the general ideals underlying the group's Weltanschauung.

77   "Everyone who wishes to join the community must pledge himself to . . . live according to the communal rule . . . [and] to do what is good and upright in . . . [God's] sight, in accordance with what He has commmanded through Moses and . . . the prophets."

Section 3 embodies an encapsulated idea of the nature of God.

78   "All that is and ever was comes from a God of knowledge."

Although God is taken to be one, chapter 3 illustrates the group's concomitant belief in a duo of subordinate spirits.

79   ". . . God . . . appointed for . . . [man] two
        spirits after whose direction he was to
        walk . . . . They are the spirits of truth and of
        perversity.
             ". . . All who practice righteousness are
        under the domination of the Prince of
        Lights, . . . whereas all who practice perver-
        sity are under the domination of the Angel of
        Darkness . . . .
             "Howbeit, the God of Israel and the Angel of
        His truth are always there to help the sons of
        light."

That the forces of light will in due time vanquish the
forces of darkness, is a further teaching of the Manual's
section 3.

80   "God in His inscrutable wisdom has ap-
        pointed a term for the existence of perversity,
        and when the time . . . comes, He will destroy
        it for ever."

Section 5 governs the manner of settling disputes
within the community.

81   "When anyone has a charge against his
        neighbor, he is to prosecute it truthfully, hum-
        bly and humanely. He is not to speak to him
        angrily or querulously or arrogantly or in any
        wicked mood."

Section 9 admonishes each member of the community
to accept with equanimity whatever happens.

82   "He is to accept willingly whatever befalls
        him and to take pleasure in nothing but the will
        of God."

III
THE APOCRYPHA

Beginning about 200 B.C.E., while many of the books comprising the Hebrew Bible were being compiled, edited, and recognized as canonical, approximately fifteen additional books relating to the Jewish religion were composed—in Hebrew, Aramaic, or Greek.

These books came to be called Apocrypha (Hidden Items), because the rabbis did not recognize them as warranting inclusion in the category of Sacred Scriptures. Varying degrees of acceptance of the Apocrypha evolved as follows:

— The Jewish-sponsored principal Greek translation of the Hebrew Bible—the Septuagint—included most of the Apocryphal books, interspersing them among the regular books of the Bible.

— The Christian-sponsored Latin translation of the Old and New Testaments, which was made by Saint Jerome, also included some of these books, again interspersing them among the books of the Old Testament.

— Differences arose among Christian groups—Roman Catholic, Eastern Orthodox, Coptic, Ethiopian, and Protestant—as to which of the Apocryphal books should be reverenced and where they should be placed in the Bible. Some editions or translations placed these books in a group, located between the Old and New Testaments.

— As a result, it is almost necessary to examine individual editions in order to determine how the Apocrypha are viewed by a given religious group. (Reportedly, the Bible on which British monarchs take the oath of office contains some portions of the Apocrypha.)

— Jewish editions or translations of the Bible, after the Septuagint, generally exclude the Apocrypha. But the Ethiopian Jews, who are sometimes called Falashas, have an expanded canon, which includes some Apocryphal books.

A. The Wisdom of Solomon

The Apocryphal book entitled The Wisdom of Solomon states that it was written by King Solomon, but even Saint Jerome rejected that proposition. The text which we have of this book is written in Greek, but our text may be a translation from an original which was in Hebrew.

In the first chapter of this Apocryphal work, the following is said regarding wisdom.

83   "[W]isdom will not enter into a soul that deviseth evil, nor dwell in a body that is held in pledge by sin."

Chapter 5 declares that the sinful way of life is as "chaff carried by the wind."

84   "We took our fill of the paths of lawlessness and destruction, and we journeyed through trackless deserts, but the way of the Lord we knew not.

"What did our arrogancy profit us? And what good have riches and vaunting brought us?

"Those things all passed away as a shadow, . . . as a ship passing through the billowing water, whereof, when it is gone by, there is no trace to be found, . . .

"Because the hope of the ungodly man is as chaff carried by the wind, and as foam vanishing before a tempest; . . . and passeth by as the remembrance of a guest that tarrieth but a day."

Chapter 7 describes the wisdom which the author received through God's grace.

85   "I called upon God, and there came to me a spirit of wisdom. . . .

"[And wisdom taught me] an unerring knowledge of the things that are, to know the constitution of the world, and the operation of the elements; . . . the circuits of years and the positions of stars; the natures of living creatures . . . and the thoughts of men, . . . for she that is the artificer of all things taught me, even wisdom."

B. Ecclesiasticus

Another Apocryphal book which emphasizes wisdom is (unlike The Wisdom of Solomon) known to have been written originally in Hebrew, but we have now, besides a full translation into Greek, only fragments of the basic Hebrew text.

The Greek title of the work is translatable as The Wisdom of Jesus, Son of Sirach. It soon began to be called, however, The Wisdom of Ben Sira (Son of Sirach); and then, from the fourth century C.E., when the book was used in sermons spoken in churches, the name Ecclesiasticus ("For Use in Church") became attached to this work.

Some of the maxims of Ben Sira are quoted in the Talmud (by rabbis who in general did not recognize the Apocrypha as Holy Writ) and in the New Testament as well.

Chapter 1 discusses wisdom in general, as a personified spirit, as illustrated above in a passage from The Wisdom of Solomon.

86   "The sand of the seas, and the drops of rain, and the days of eternity, who shall number? The height of the heaven, and the breadth of the earth, and the deep, and wisdom, who shall search them out?

"Wisdom hath been created before all things, and the understanding of prudence from everlasting."

Chapter 1 continues with a point that wisdom teaches, namely, the importance of the fear of the Lord.

87   "The fear of the Lord is glory, and exultation,
          and gladness, and a crown of rejoicing. . . .
          The fear of the Lord is the beginning of wis-
          dom."

Chapter 44 contains an apt expression which has become a byword.

88   "Let us now praise famous men, and our
          fathers that begat us. . . . Such as . . . were
          renowned for their power, giving counsel by
          their understanding, . . . men of learning for
          the people; wise were their words in their in-
          struction: . . . all these were honoured in their
          generations, and were a glory in their days."

IV
THE PSEUDEPIGRAPHA

Besides the Scriptural-type documents which came to be called the Apocrypha, numerous other such texts, which in general are noncanonical, date from the period beginning about 200 B.C.E. The first serious effort to collect these supplementary texts was made by J.A. Fabricius, of Hungary, who lived from 1678 to 1734. His collection, limited at first to Jewishly-oriented texts associated with the Hebrew Bible, was entitled *Codex Pseudepigraphus Veteris Testamenti* (False-Writing Appendix of the Old Testament).

Since the time of Fabricius, additional texts of the same kind have been identified and assembled, and they have continued to be called Pseudepigrapha ("False Writings"). The words "False Writings," however, mean not that the substantive content of the books is false but that their ascription to designated persons (Adam, Abraham, Moses, Ezra, Daniel, etc.) as their authors, is false.

A. Apocalypse of Baruch

Many books written in the period from 200 B.C.E. to 200 C.E. are called "apocalypses"; that is, books purporting to contain revelations from heaven. Two such books are (falsely) ascribed to Baruch, a scribe who lived in the seventh and sixth centuries B.C.E. Of the two Apocalypses of Baruch, one was included in the semi-holy Apocrypha; the other—designated as 2 Baruch—is a part of the Pseudepigrapha.

This book, 2 Baruch, was written in Hebrew, but what we have today is a translation of it into the Syriac language. The book conveys a picture of an idyllic future era.

89   "And it will happen that after he [God] . . . has sat down in eternal peace on the throne of the kingdom, then joy will be revealed and rest will appear.

"And . . . health will descend in dew, and
illness will vanish, and fear and tribulation and
lamentation will pass away from among men,
. . .
"And women will no longer have pain when
they bear, nor will they be tormented when
they yield the fruits of their womb."

B. Ethiopic Book of Enoch

Another book describing a future time of peace and joy
is one of the three books ascribed by their authors to
Enoch, the son of Cain. Of these three books, the first
(composed between 200 B.C.E. and 100 C.E.) is sometimes called 1 Enoch. It was written either entirely in
Hebrew or Aramaic, or partly in each. What has survived, however, is an Ethiopic translation.

This book is mentioned in the New Testament and was
regarded as canonical by some early church fathers.

90   "[E]very iniquitous deed will end, and the
        plant of righteousness and truth will appear
        . . . .
        "And the earth shall be cleansed from all pol-
        lution, and from all . . . suffering.
        "And peace and truth shall become partners
        . . . in all . . . generations."

In the foregoing pages, constituting Part One of the
present work, we have savored the enchanting intellectual delights proffered by an array of indescribably great
poets, prophets, and sages of the Scriptural era. In Part
Two, we shall continue our pursuit of such delights in
the post-Scriptural period.

Part Two

NUGGETS OF WISDOM
FROM RABBINICAL AND OTHER
POST-SCRIPTURAL DISCUSSIONS

I
THE TALMUD

The word "Talmud" means Study. Fittingly, therefore, the document entitled "The Talmud" is a record of centuries of rabbinical *study*, in the form of

> hypotheses and counter-hypotheses,
> argument and counter-argument,
> development and evaluation of evidence, and
> imaginative speculation,

about how the world operates and how people should live.

Viewing the Talmud in the perspective of its two components—the Mishnah (Learning) and the Gemara (Tradition)—I offer here resplendent passages from one tractate of the Mishnah, namely, "Abot" (Fathers), and from several tractates of the Gemara.

1. The Mishnah

The Mishnah is a collection of sixty-three "tractates," or treatises, each of which displays the "Learning" of recognized sages on a specific subject. Perhaps the most revered of these tractates is the one entitled "Abot" (sometimes called Chapters of the Fathers, or Ethics of the Fathers), which contains some of the most appealing ethical pronouncements in the entire Mishnah. A portion of "Abot" is read in many synagogues every Sabbath afternoon during the spring and summer.

Chapter I

Chapter I, section 1, of "Abot" contains the following momentous declaration:

91   "The men of the Great Assembly said three things: Be deliberate in judgment, raise many disciples, and make a hedge about the Torah."

Paralleling the "three things" emphasized in section 1,

we find in section 2 another triple listing of exceptionally weighty factors, as follows:

92   "Simeon the Righteous used to say: On three things the age stands—on Torah, on the Temple service, and on acts of piety."

Since the aim of wisdom-seekers is to "drink in" the words of ancient sages, section 4 of the first chapter of "Abot" is especially relevant. It reads:

93   "Jose ben Joezer says: Let thy house be a meeting-place for sages, and sit in the very dust at their feet, and thirstily drink in their words."

Skipping, in chapter 1 of "Abot," to section 15, we learn of still another triple grouping of ideas. Section 15 reads:

94   "Shammai says: Make thy study of the Torah a fixed practice; say little and do much; and receive all men with a cheerful countenance."

A different theme, praise of silence, is emphasized in section 17, where we learn the following:

95   "Simeon, . . . [Gamaliel's] son, says: All my life I grew up among the sages and have found nothing better for anybody than silence."

In section 18, we encounter one more grouping of three things of importance, namely:

96   "Rabban Simeon ben Gamaliel says: By three things is the world sustained: by justice, by truth, and by peace."

Chapter II

Turning to chapter II of "Abot," we are confronted at the very beginning (in section 1) with the following additional trio of profound ideas:

97   "Rabbi [that is, Judah the prince, compiler of the Mishnah] says: Know what is above thee—

an eye that sees, an ear that hears, and all thine
actions recorded in a book."

Section 1 of chapter II, as just stated, quotes a saying by
Judah the Prince. Section 2 of this chapter quotes a saying
by the son of Judah the Prince, as follows:

98   "Rabbi Gamaliel, the son of Rabbi Judah the
        Prince, says: Splendid is the study of Torah
        when combined with a worldly occupation, for
        toil in them both puts sin out of mind."

Section 5 quotes the celebrated sage Hillel on two
salutary ideas:

99   "Hillel says: Do not judge thy comrade until
        thou hast stood in his place. . . .
        "And say not: 'When I have leisure I will
        study'—perchance thou shalt have no leisure."

Section 6 offers another saying by Hillel, which is often
cited:

100   "[Hillel] used to say: . . . Where there are no
        men, strive to be a man."

In section 11, we read an edifying injunction that is
puzzling when one first reads it:

101   "Rabbi Eliezer says: . . . Repent one day be-
        fore thy death."

An explanatory comment on this strange dictum will
be presented shortly in our section on the Gemara. But
you can probably guess the answer to the question, How
can I know the day before my death? (The answer is: Repent every day.)

Two interrelated sayings by Rabbi Tarfon are found in
sections 15 and 16 of the second chapter of "Abot." In
section 15, we read this exciting series of propositions:

102   "Rabbi Tarfon says: The day is short, the
        work is plentiful, . . . the reward is abundant,
        and the master of the house presses."

This series of propositions is reminiscent of the
aphorism of Hippocrates, "Life is short, and art long; the

crisis fleeting, experience perilous, and decision difficult."

Rabbi Tarfon, I said, is also quoted in section 16. That
section reads:

103   "Rabbi Tarfon used to say: It is not thy duty
to finish the work, but thou art not at liberty to
neglect it."

Chapter III

I turn now to "Abot," chapter III. In section 1 of chapter III, we learn of the spiritual significance of studying
Torah:

104   "Rabbi Hananiah ben Teradyon says: If two
sit together, and the words between them are
not of Torah, then that is a session of scorn-
ers, . . . but if two sit together and the words
between them *are* of Torah, then the
Shekhinah [Divine Spirit] is in their midst. . . .
"Even when *one* sits studying the Torah, the
Holy One, blessed be He, fixes a reward for
him."

Chapter III, section 8, of "Abot" presents the first of
two opposite answers, which I have extracted from the
Talmud, to the question, Should we stop to smell the
flowers? (This question is important in today's competi-
tive, achievement-oriented societies.) Section 8 of chapter III contains a negative answer to the question. It reads
as follows:

105   "If one is studying as he walks along the
highway, and he interrupts his study and
exclaims, 'How handsome is this tree, how
handsome this field!', Scripture [Deuterono-
my, chapter 4, verse 9] accounts it to him as
though he were mortally guilty."

The verse in Deuteronomy which is here invoked in
opposition to taking time to smell the flowers reads, in
part, ". . . keep thy soul diligently, lest thou forget the

things which thine eyes have seen." We shall soon see, however, that a later pronouncement in the Talmud offers support for stopping to smell the flowers.

I ask you now to restrain your curiosity, and hold it in abeyance for a few minutes, until we reach that opposite nugget of wisdom, since we are proceeding through the Talmud in the numerical sequence of its parts, not a topical sequence.

We are still in chapter III of "Abot" in our march through the Talmud. Section 16 of chapter III is the source of a famous putdown of those who argue that human beings cannot have free will if God knows all of their actions beforehand. Section 16 says:

106   "Everything is foreseen, yet freedom of choice is granted."

Chapter IV

Chapter IV of "Abot" offers, in section 4, the following thought on humility:

107   "Rabbi Levitas of Yavneh says: Be of an exceedingly humble spirit, for the end of man is the worm."

Chapter V

I shall now quote two sections of chapter V of "Abot." Section 7 reads as follows:

108   "Seven qualities characterize the clod and seven the wise man; the wise man does not speak before him that is greater than he in wisdom; he does not break into his fellow's speech; he is not in a rush to reply; he asks what is relevant and replies to the point; he speaks of first things first and of last things last; of what he has not heard he says: 'I have not heard'; and he acknowledges what is true.
    "And the opposite applies to the clod."

The other section of chapter V which is to be quoted here is section 20. It says, in beguiling metaphors:

109   "Judah ben Tema says: Be strong as the leopard, swift as the eagle, fleet as the gazelle, and brave as the lion, to do the will of thy Father who is in heaven."

Chapter VI

From chapter VI, section 6, of "Abot," I quote a maxim which I am obeying in this volume:

110   ". . . whoever quotes his source brings deliverance to the world."

2. The Gemara

As noted above, "Mishnah" means Learning, and "Gemara" means Tradition. What we find in the Gemara, therefore, is the Tradition of memorable rabbinical elaborations of the Mishnah.

There are, however, two Gemaras—one contained in the Babylonian Talmud and the other contained in the Palestinian Talmud. Except where otherwise noted, all of my quotations from the Gemara are taken from the Babylonian version.

In the case of the Mishnah, I quoted passages from only one tractate, namely, "Abot." Now, I shall quote noteworthy passages from the Gemara's comments on ten separate Mishnah tractates. I shall take up the Gemara passages on these ten Mishnah tractates in alphabetical order according to the Hebrew names of the Mishnah tractates on which they comment (Abodah Zarah, Arakhin, Baba Metzia, Berakhot, etc.).

For each quotation in English from the Gemara of the Babylonian Talmud (commenting on a passage in the corresponding Mishnah tractate), I shall indicate the number of the page—in the standard Hebrew printed text of each tractate of the Babylonian Talmud—where the Gemara quotation appears. (This corresponds to my citation of the chapters and sections in my quotations from the Mishnah tractate "Abot.")

For my quotations from the Gemara of the Palestinian Talmud, I shall cite either the number of the page or the chapter and the section, depending on the citation in the sources that I used.

Abodah Zarah

Let us begin our selections from the Gemara with the Gemara on the Mishnah tractate "Abodah Zarah" (Idolatry). In the Gemara regarding that Mishnah tractate, on page 20a of the standard Hebrew text, an important blessing is recorded:

111   "He who sees goodly creatures says: Blessed is He in whose world are such creatures as these."

Arakhin

The Gemara on the Mishnah tractate "Arakhin" (Vows of Valuation), on page 15b of the Hebrew text, instructs us on the evil effects of slander:

112   "[Slander] slays three persons: the speaker, the spoken to, and the spoken of."

Baba Metzia

A fascinating story is told in the Gemara on the Mishnah tractate "Baba Metzia" (Middle Gate), page 8c.

113   "Rabbi Samuel bar Susreta went up to Rome, [where he found an ornament which the queen had lost and about which the authorities had proclaimed a reward for its return *within* thirty days and punishment in the form of decapitation for its return *after* thirty days. Bar Susreta returned the ornament *after* thirty days. When the queen asked him to explain, he replied:] 'That you might not say I did it out of fear of you, but rather out of fear of God.'

"She said to him: Blessed be the God of the Jews."

Berakhot

I now offer you four noble passages from the Gemara on the Mishnah tractate "Berakhot" (Blessings). The first of these four passages appears on page 7a:

114   "How do we know that the Holy One, praised be He, prays? It is written, 'I will bring them to My holy mountain and make them rejoice in My house of prayer' (Isaiah, chapter 56, verse 7). This verse states not '*their* house of prayer' but '*My* house of prayer,' from which we infer that the Holy One, praised be He, prays. What is His prayer? Rav Tuviah bar Zutra, quoting Rav [Abba Areka], said, 'May it be My will that My compassion overcome My wrath, and that it prevail over My attribute of strict justice.'"

The second of my four selections from the Gemara on the Mishnah tractate "Berakhot" appears on page 10a:

115   "As the Holy One, blessed be He, fills the whole world, so also the soul fills the whole body.
       "As the Holy One, blessed be He, sees but cannot be seen, so also the soul sees but cannot be seen."

The third of my four extracts from the Gemara on the Mishnah tractate "Berakhot" reads as follows (page 28b):

116   ". . . when you are praying, remember before Whom you are standing."

Lastly, the Gemara on the Mishnah tractate "Berakhot" contains, on page 33b, the following pungent remark on the problem of human freedom:

117   "[Rabbi Hanina said:] Everything is in the power of Heaven except the fear of Heaven."

Kiddushin

Next, I quote three glorious passages from the Gemara on the Mishnah tractate "Kiddushin" (Betrothals). The first of the three comes from the Palestinian Talmud. This is the passage that you have been impatiently waiting for, the *affirmative* view on the question, Should we stop to smell the flowers? (The negative view, you will remember, was expressed in the Mishnah tractate "Abot.") The affirmative view, in the Gemara on the Mishnah tractate "Kiddushin," reads (chapter 4, section 12):

118   ". . . man will be called to *account* for all the delights which he *missed*, though he had the opportunity to enjoy them."

My second selection from the Gemara on the Mishnah tractate "Kiddushin" comes from pages 30b-31a. It reads:

119   "Rabbi Joseph, when he heard the sound of his mother's steps, said: 'I shall rise before the Divine Presence which is coming.'"

The third selection from the Gemara on the Mishnah tractate "Kiddushin" is as follows (page 61d, Palestinian Talmud):

120   "Though nine hundred and ninety-nine angels attest for a man's conviction, and only one angel attests for his defense, the Holy One, blessed be He, inclines the scales in his favour."

Pesachim

Two passages are now to be presented from the Gemara on another Mishnah tractate, "Pesachim" (Passover). First (page 25b):

121   "A man once came before Raba [Rabbi ben Joseph ben Hama] and said to him: 'The ruler of my city has ordered me to kill a certain person, and if I refuse he will kill me.' Raba told him, 'Be killed and do not kill; do you think that your blood is redder than his? Perhaps his blood is redder than yours.'"

The position taken by Raba is similar to that taken by Socrates when the Athenian "Thirty Tyrants" ordered him to seize a resident of Salamis whom they wanted to put to death. Socrates defied the order, and the Tyrants were soon ousted.

My second selection from the Gemara on the Mishnah tractate "Pesachim" (page 99a) echoes a sentiment quoted above (from the Mishnah) about silence:

122   "Silence is good for the wise; how much more so for the foolish!"

Sanhedrin

Here is a notable injunction recorded in the Gemara on the Mishnah tractate "Sanhedrin" (Assembly), page 74a:

123   "If a person is required to transgress all the ordinances of the Torah under threat of being put to death, he may do so with the exception of those relating to idolatry, immorality, and bloodshed."

Shabbat

From the Gemara on the Mishnah tractate "Shabbat" (Sabbath), I offer you four touching excerpts. First (page 14c):

124   "The evil impulse is at first sweet; in the end it is bitter.

Second (page 31a):

125   "Hillel . . . [when asked by a would-be con- vert to teach him the Torah while standing on one leg] said to him: what is hateful to you, do not do to your fellow. That is all the Torah. The rest is commentary."

Third (page 88):

126   "When Moses ascended to heaven . . . to receive the Torah, the ministering angels . . . [demurred. God having invited Moses to speak to them, Moses said:]

        "[1. Respecting 'I am the Lord thy God who brought thee out of the land of Egypt'] Did *you*

go down to Egypt? Were *you* enslaved by
Pharoah?

"[2. Respecting 'Thou shalt have no other
gods'] Are *you* surrounded by nations that
worship other gods?

"[Etc., referring to the other components of
the Decalogue].

"At once they conceded."

My fourth and last passage from the Gemara on the
Mishnah tractate "Shabbat" (page 153a) refers to the injunction, quoted earlier, to repent the day before you die:

127   "Rabbi Eliezer said: 'Turn to God the day before you die.'

"And his disciples asked him: 'Does a man
know on what day he will die?'

"And he answered them, saying: 'Just because of this, let him turn to God on this *very*
day, . . . and thus it will come about that *all* his
days will be days of turning to God.'"

Taanit

From the Gemara on the Mishnah tractate "Taanit"
(Days of Fasting), page 7a, here is an important insight
on teaching and learning:

128   "Rabbi Hanina said: Much have I learned
from my masters, and more from my comrades
than from my masters, and from my disciples
the most."

Yebamot

The Gemara on the Mishnah tractate "Yebamot" (Sis-
ters-in-Law) tells us the following about prayer (page
64a):

129   "The Holy One, praised be He, longs for the
prayers of the righteous."

I shall complete this section on the Gemara by quoting four memorable Gemara passages published in English by the anthologist Philip Birnbaum, who, however, did not indicate the specific tractates from which he had selected these passages.

130   "If the pupil makes progress, good and well;
        if not, put him next to a studious companion."

131   "Men should be careful not to give their
        wives any cause for tears, for God counts their
        tears."

132   "Teach your tongue to say: 'I do not know.'"

133   "If two men ask for your help and one of
        them is your enemy, help your enemy first."

II
THE MIDRASH

The Talmud, as a monument of post-Biblical Jewish wisdom, was supplemented by rabbinical writings constituting a further corpus of Jewish wisdom known as the Midrash (Research). The elements of the Midrash in which I have found uplifting passages worth quoting are as follows:

1. Additions to the Mishnah
   A. Abot de-Rabbi Natan
   B. Tosefta

2. Commentaries on specific books of the Bible
   A. Midrash Rabbah
   B. Others

3. Commentaries on the portions of the Pentateuch to be read on successive Sabbaths
   A. Pesikta de-Rav Kahana
   B. Tanhuma

Additions to the Mishnah

Abot de-Rabbi Natan. From "Abot de-Rabbi Natan" (The Fathers According to Rabbi Nathan), I shall quote three excerpts—two which appear in both of the extant versions of that work, and one which appears *only* in version B.

Of the two selected insights which appear in both versions, here is the first:

134   "Seven qualities avail before the Throne of Glory: faith, righteousness, justice, loving-kindness, mercy, truth, and peace."

The second one asserts:

135   "Not study is the chief thing, but action."

The selected insight which appears only in version B of "Abot de-Rabbi Natan" has often been anthologized. It reads:

136   "If there be a plant in your hand when they
       say to you: Behold the Messiah!—Go and plant
       the plant, and afterward go out to greet him."

With the foregoing quotation we may compare the Islamic saying, "If planting a date tree when the Day of Judgment arrives, go on with your planting!"

"Abot de-Rabbi Natan," from which I have just presented some trenchant quotations, constitutes the first of my two listed "additions" to the Mishnah. I turn now to the second such addition, namely, the collection known as the Tosefta (Addition).

Tosefta. This body of doctrinal pronouncements is arranged in tractates corresponding to the tractates of the original Mishnah. The Tosefta, however, is five times as large as the original Mishnah.

I plan to quote only three extracts from the Tosefta. First, we read the following in the Tosefta's additions to the Mishnah tractate "Baba Kamma" (First Gate):

137   "More serious is the defrauding of a non-Jew
       than the defrauding of a brother Israelite, on
       account of the profanation of the Name."

My second offering in this category is an addition in the Tosefta to the Mishnah tractate "Kiddushin" (Betrothals), as follows:

138   ". . . whoever does not teach his son a trade
       teaches him to become a robber."

My last offering in this category is an addition in the Tosefta to the Mishnah tractate "Shebuot" (Oaths), namely:

139   ". . . nobody proceeds to commit a trans-
       gression without first having denied Him who
       prohibited it."

Commentaries on Specific
Books of the Bible

In my outline of components of the Midrash, I listed additions to the Mishnah (a category which we have now covered, if only briefly), commentaries on specific books of the Bible, and commentaries on the weekly portions of the Pentateuch.

Commentaries on specific books of the Bible include (1) those constituting the Midrash Rabbah and (2) a variety of others.

From the Midrash Rabbah, I shall quote nuggets of wisdom from Genesis Rabbah, Exodus Rabbah, Leviticus Rabbah, and Deuteronomy Rabbah.

Genesis Rabbah. This component of the Midrash contains in chapter 3 the following interesting speculation:

140   "Other worlds were created and destroyed ere the present one was decided on as a permanent one."

A comparable speculation is found in (1) Indian thought about a periodic destruction and renewal of the world and (2) the Stoic view that at certain fated periods the world is dissolved by fire and again formed into a world.

In chapter 8 of Genesis Rabbah, we are told the following story:

141   "When the Holy One, blessed be He, came to create the first man, He foresaw that both righteous and wicked [descendants] would issue from him. He said, 'If I create him, wicked men will issue from him; if I do not create him, how can righteous men spring from him?'"

Chapter 10 of Genesis Rabbah suggests an explanation of the existence of annoying insects:

142   "Even such things as you deem superfluous in the world, e.g. flies, fleas, and gnats, are necessary parts of the cosmic order and were created by the Holy One, blessed be He, for his purpose—yea, even serpents and frogs."

The Jain religion also asserts that, in the cosmic plan, insects have a right to life.

In Genesis Rabbah, chapter 34, we learn of seven commandments which preceded the Decalogue, as follows:

143   "The sons of Noah were given seven commandments, forbidding idolatry, adultery, bloodshed, profaning God's name, injustice, robbery, and cutting the flesh or a limb from a living animal."

Here is what Genesis Rabbah says about helping the poor (chapter 61):

144   "If a poor man comes to thee for aid in the morning, give it to him. If he comes again in the evening, give it to him once more."

Later chapters of Genesis Rabbah give us two further valuable insights. First:

145   "Wherever the righteous go, the Shechinah [Divine Spirit] goes with them."

In the last of our golden nuggets from Genesis Rabbah, we discover the following about marriages:

146   "A Roman lady asked a Rabbi, '. . . What has . . . [God] been doing since . . . [creation]?' [The Rabbi replied,] 'He has been arranging marriages.'"

Exodus Rabbah. From Exodus Rabbah, here is a description of the giving of the Torah:

147   "When the Holy One, blessed be He, gave the Torah, not a bird cried; not a fowl flew; not an ox bellowed; the angels did not fly; the seraphim did not say, Holy, Holy; the sea did not stir; the human creatures did not speak; . . . the world was still and silent."

Leviticus Rabbah. Leviticus Rabbah includes a number of inspirational insights, of which I here quote three. First:

148   "When Adam heard . . . [Cain say, 'I repented, and I am pardoned,' Adam] said, 'Is the power of repentance as great as that? I did not know it was so.'"

My second and third selections from Leviticus Rabbah concern helping the poor.

149   "More than the householder does for the beggar, the beggar does for the householder."

150   "When the beggar stands at your door, the Holy One, blessed be He, stands at his right hand."

Deuteronomy Rabbah. My next two pronouncements on the best way of life are taken from Deuteronomy Rabbah.

151   "The gates of prayer are sometimes open and sometimes closed but the gates of repentance are always open."

152   ". . . take care not to pervert justice, for by so doing you shake the world."

Midrashic commentaries on specific books of the Bible—besides the above-illustrated components of Midrash Rabbah—include the Midrash on Psalms, the Midrash on the Song of Songs, and the Midrash on Ecclesiastes.

Psalms. In the Midrash on Psalms, we read:

153   "Repentance is of no avail in a matter of wronging your fellow man, without first rectifying the wrong done."

Song of Songs. The Midrash on the Song of Songs states:

154   "The Holy One, blessed be He, said to Israel, My sons, open for Me an aperture of repentance as narrow as the eye of a needle, and I will open for you gates through which wagons and coaches can pass."

Ecclesiastes. Concern over the preservation of the environment is dealt with in the Midrash on Ecclesiastes, where we may read:

155   "When the Holy One, blessed be He, created the first man, He took him and warned him about all the trees of the Garden of Eden, saying:

"See My works, how beautiful and perfect
they are;
    "Beware lest you spoil and destroy My
world, for if you spoil it, there is no one to re-
pair it for you."

Commentaries on the Weekly
Portions of the Pentateuch

I end this garland of pious and worldly wisdom with
passages from two Midrashic commentaries on the portions of the Torah designated for reading on successive
Sabbaths, (1) the Pesikta de-Rav Kahana and (2) the
Tanhuma.

Pesikta de-Rav Kahana. The first of my final two passages is taken from the "Pesikta de-Rav Kahana."
("Pesikta" means "Portions." "Rav" is a variant form of
"Rabbi.") In this Midrash on the portions of the week, we
find the following provocative thought:

156   "The nations of the world . . . [considered
        attacking a certain country. On seeking advice,
        they were told]: Go and pass before their
        Houses of Study and Houses of Prayer. If you
        there hear children chanting, you cannot at-
        tack them."

Tanhuma. The last of my selections from Midrashic
commentaries on the portions of the Torah designated
for reading on successive Sabbaths is from the Midrash
known as "Tanhuma." According to this Midrash,

157   "At Sinai, the women received and accepted
        the Decalogue before the men."

The Midrash which you have just read, on the exalted
role of women at Sinai, may assuage the disquiet which
feminists among my readers may have felt over the repeated use, in my selections, of the word "men" as referring to all human beings.

III

THE PHILOSOPHY OF PHILO JUDAEUS

The concern of Jews in Asia Minor with the Talmud and the Midrash endured for several centuries. Meanwhile, in nearby Egypt, thousands of Jews found new homes during the hegemony over Palestine of Persia, Greece, and Rome.

Alexandria in Egypt became the center of a lively Jewish community. In it, Philo Judaeus (Philo the Jew) lived from about 20 B.C.E. to 50 C.E. His spoken and written language was Greek, and he was familiar with the writings of the great Greek philosophers and writers. In addition, he became steeped in Jewish traditions, and he knew the Bible thoroughly, though perhaps in a Greek translation. He visited Rome and Jerusalem.

Philo's thinking is a combination of Stoicism, Platonism, and Judaism. His views on the Jewish religion lean toward an allegorical interpretation of much of the Hebrew Bible, especially in relation to Biblical references to the hand of God, the voice of God, etc.

In continuance of my occasional presentation of nuggets of wisdom which are *about wisdom*, I shall quote from one of Philo's Biblical commentaries ("On the Migration of Abraham") in which he said that the pursuit of wisdom warrants the greatest effort.

158   "[F]or the sake of the most beautiful and desirable of all possessions, the only one which is peculiar to the human race, namely, wisdom, . . . [seekers should be willing] to cross over every sea and to penetrate every recess of the earth, . . . until they arrive at the enjoyment of the things which are thus sought for and desired."

In keeping with Philo's allegorical interpretation of the Bible, he belittled those Scriptural stories which report that God was angry, was sorry that he had created human beings, was vengeful or jealous, and the like. Philo wrote on this subject, in "On the Unchangeableness of God":

159   "God is utterly inaccessible to any anger or
       passion whatever. . . . [S]uch things are spo-
       ken with reference to God by the great law-
       giver . . . for the sake of admonishing those
       persons who could not be corrected other-
       wise."

In the same essay, Philo took up the matter of God's
knowledge of human occurrences, in the perspective of
eternity. On that topic, Philo defended an abtruse and
abstract conception, which further differentiated his understanding of God from the worshipful reverence for a
personal Deity which many Jews have cherished. Although Philo's conception seems "far out," many of the
well-supported doctrines of present-day physics and
cosmology are also in that category:

160   "[I]n eternity, nothing is past and nothing is
       future, but everything is present only."

As to the sense in which we may credibly assert that
God made human beings in His own image, Philo said
("On the Creation of the World"):

161   "[T]he mind which exists in each individual
       has been created after the likeness of that one
       [universal] mind which is . . . [a model for all
       other minds. Each human mind is] . . . in some
       sort the God of that body which carries it
       about."

In ethics, Philo emphasized the importance of civility,
especially on the part of the politically powerful.

162   "I will . . . behave myself in an affable, and
       courteous, and conciliatory manner to all men,
       even if I should obtain the dominion over all
       the earth."

Despite his prime concern for a clear understanding of
highly theoretical topics, Philo was also down-to-earth in
recognizing the paramount role of the sex impulse in the
affairs of living beings.

163   "[O]f all the delights which pleasure can af-
       ford, the association of man with woman is the
       most exquisite."

I close Part Two of the present work, which embodies
Nuggets of Wisdom from Rabbinical and Other Post-
Scriptural Discussions, with two appendixes, which may
be useful to those who want to learn more about the rabbinical thinking which is reported in the Talmud and the
Midrash. For more information about Philo, the best
source is the four-volume translation of his writings published in London.

In Part Three, which follows the two appendixes of
Part Two, we shall find a mine of wisdom from medieval
Jewish sages.

Appendix 1 to Part Two

TEACHERS OR RABBIS WHO WROTE OR COMPILED THE TALMUD AND THE MIDRASH

The writers and compilers of the Talmud and the Midrash flourished in the first several centuries of the common era. Their work was preceded, however, by teachers in two preliminary groups. (Years shown in this appendix are rounded approximations.)

Preliminary Groups

The teachers in these preliminary groups—called "sopherim" (scribes)—began the centuries-long process of rendering oral interpretations of Scripture, deciding, for example, that the commandment to rest on the Sabbath forbids engaging in business on that day. These teachers consisted of:

(1) The Men of the Great Synagogue (500-200 B.C.E.), who determined what was sacred enough to be included in the Bible and who were early developers of the synagogue service.

(2) The Sanhedrin (mentioned disparagingly in the New Testament), which was headed until about 30 C.E. by *zugot* (pairs), two of whom (Hillel and Shammai) are mentioned below. The Sanhedrin added oral decisions to those of the previous sopherim, the cumulation of such decisions leading to a split between the Pharisees, who accepted the developing oral tradition in detail, and the Sadducees, who rejected the post-Biblical oral tradition.

Tannaim

The principal crystallizers of Jewish doctrinal positions in the first two centuries of the common era were called "tannaim" (those who "hand down orally"). They were primarily developers of the Mishnah.

Hillel and Shammai. Of the *zugot* mentioned above, the last were Hillel and Shammai. Hillel (first century B.C.E.) and his school were *lenient* in applying Scriptural injunctions. Shammai (50 B.C.E. to 30 C.E.) and his school were *strict* in interpreting scripture.

Prominent Tannaim After Hillel and Shammai. Among those who were active in handing down the tradition or in rendering new decisions were:

> (1) Johanan ben Zakkai (50), who supported the Pharisaic view on accepting the oral tradition.
>
> (2) Gamaliel I (50), grandson of Hillel and teacher of Paul (Acts 5:34).
>
> (3) Akiva (50-135), who compiled the oral tradition into an early version of the Mishnah.
>
> (4) Judah ha-Nasi (175-225), great-grandson of Gamaliel I; compiler of the Mishnah.

Amoraim

The chief developers of the Gemara (200-500) were called "amoraim" (spokesmen). During their deliberations about the written and oral tradition, the distinction arose between

> (1) *peshat*, which meant either the literal meaning (which is what Rashi in the eleventh century took it to mean) or, if not literal, at least an *accepted* derivative meaning, and
>
> (2) *derash*, which referred to an imaginative, story-oriented or sermon-oriented (homiletic) meaning.

This distinction is related to that between *halakhic* interpretation (law), which is prominent in the Mishnah, and *aggadic* interpretation (lore), which is prominent in the Gemara.

Savoraim

In Babylon, 500-550, the savoraim (competent scholars) put the finishing touches on the Babylonian Talmud.

STRUCTURAL COMPONENTS OF
THE TALMUD AND THE MIDRASH

I. The Talmud

The Talmud consists of two elements, one legalistic and the other folkloristic, as follows:

> (A) the Mishnah, made up primarily of halakhic (legal) texts;
> (B) the Gemara, made up largely of aggadic material (lore rather than law).

In addition, mention must be made of (C) Talmudic compendiums and commentaries. Outlined below are the basic facts about the three items cited here as A, B, and C.

A. *Mishnah.* This portion of the Talmud consists of sixty-three tractates, each dealing with a specific subject. After Judah ha-Nasi had completed it, this compilation was anonymously revised, to include, for example, Judah ha-Nasi's own opinions. Slightly different versions of the Mishnah were used in the preparation of the two Gemaras.

B. *Gemara.* By nature, the Gemara is a commentary on the Mishnah. Of the Gemara, there are two versions, one prepared in Palestine and one in Babylonia.

> 1. Chronologically, the earlier of the two is the Gemara compiled in Palestine by Rabbi Johanan (275) and disciples, primarily in Tiberias (northern Palestine). It is incorrectly called the "Jerusalem Gemara." This Gemara covers thirty-nine of the sixty-three tractates of the Mishnah. It was written in the Western Aramaic language, which is a vernacular version of the classical Hebrew.

> 2. The second Gemara was compiled in Babylonia by Rav Ashi (400) and disciples. In time, it virtually superseded the Palestinian

Gemara. When one refers to the Babylonian Talmud, one means the Mishnah with the Babylonian Gemara. Although this Gemara covers only thirty-six of the Mishnah tractates (while the Palestinian Gemara covers thirty-nine), this Gemara is six times as large as the one prepared in Palestine. It was written in Eastern Aramaic (akin to the Syriac language, which was an important medium of communication in that era.)

C. *Talmudic compendiums and commentaries.* Six items require mention here. Numbers 1 to 3 are compendiums. The others are commentaries.

1. The work by Maimonides (1135-1204) called "Mishneh Torah" or "Yad Hakhazakah."

2. The work by Jacob ben Asher (1270?-1340) called "Arba'ah Turim," which (unlike the "Mishneh Torah") cites sources.

3. The work by Joseph Karo (1488-1575) called "Shulkhan Arukh," which was edited by Moses Isserles (1500) to show Ashkenazic practices (mainly of European Jews) where they differed from Sephardic practices (mainly of Oriental Jews).

4. The commentary on the Gemara prepared by Rabbi Solomon ben Isaac (Rashi, 1040-1105). It is included in printed editions of the Talmud, in a column near the binding; it appears in a script known as "Rashi script."

5. An anonymous collection of comments (compiled 1150 ff.) which are called "Tosafot" (Additions). These were originally additions to Rashi's commentary. They are printed in editions of the Talmud, in a column near the outer edge of the page, usually in Rashi script.

6. Other commentaries, printed in narrow columns and small type, in editions of the Talmud.

II. The Midrash

The main categories of material called "Midrash" (Research) are:

A. Additions to the Mishnah
B. Commentaries on specific books of the Bible
C. Commentaries on the portions of the Pentateuch to be read on successive Sabbaths
D. Miscellaneous other Midrashim.

A. The documents listed here as *Midrashic additions to the Mishnah* are categorized by some scholars not as parts of the Midrash but as appendages to the Mishnah. The principal documents of this kind are:

(1) A tractate entitled "Abot de-Rabbi Natan," which is a supplement to the Mishnaic tractate "Abot." Physically, this tractate appears, in the manuscripts of the Babylonian Gemara, at the end of one of the sections of the Gemara. Two versions of Abot de-Rabbi Natan exist.

(2) Tractates on the writing of Torah scrolls and on the text of the Bible ("Sopherim"); on procedures for mourning (euphemistically called "Semakhot," Joys); and on the conduct of life ("Derekh Eretz," Way of Earth).

(3) A collection called "Tosefta," which is arranged in tractates corresponding to the Mishnah. This document is five times as large as the original Mishnah.

B. The second main Midrashic category consists of *commentaries on specific books of the Bible*. These may be outlined as follows:

1. On Pentateuchal books

a. Genesis
   Bereshit Rabbah (500)
   Bereshit Rabbati, by Moses ha-Darshan
      (1150)

b. Exodus
   Shemot Rabbah (1000-1100)
   Mekhilta, by Simon ben Yohai
      (100 ff.)

c. Leviticus
   Vayikra Rabbah (650)
   Sifra (750)

d. Numbers
   Bemidbar Rabbah (1150)
   Sifre (also on Deuteronomy)

e. Deuteronomy
   Devarim Rabbah (900)
   Sifre (also on Numbers)

2. On other Biblical books

a. On Samuel: Midrash Shemuel (1000)
b. On Psalms: Midrash Tehillim (1000)
c. On Proverbs: Midrash Mishle (1000)
d. On Jonah: Midrash Yonah
e. On the scrolls (these Midrashim are
   parts of Midrash Rabbah):
      On Ruth: Midrash Ruth (1150)
      On Ecclesiastes: Midrash Kohelet
      On the Song of Songs: Midrash Shir
         ha-Shirim Rabbati
      On Lamentations: Ekah Rabbati
         (650)
      On Esther: Midrash Megillat Esther

C. The third category of Midrashic material consists of
commentaries on the "sedra" (weekly portion of the
Torah, read in the synagogue each Sabbath). Of this
material, the most prominent examples are:

Pesikta
   Pesikta de-Rav Kahana
   Pesikta Rabbati (850)

Tanhuma (500-800)
Midrash Tanhuma (which corresponds 90 percent
to the above-mentioned Devarim Rabbah)
Yelammedenu

Midrash Hashkem

D. The fourth and last category of Midrashic material consists of miscellaneous items. These include (1) individual books, commenting on the Bible or the Talmud, and (2) Midrashic anthologies.

Of the individual books, those which are most worth mentioning are:

Pirkei de Rabbi Eliezer (750)
Tanna Debe Eliahu (975)
Sefer Hayashar
Aseret ha-Dibberot (Midrash on the Ten Commandments)

Of the Midrashic anthologies, those which are best known are:

Yalkut Shimoni
Midrash Hagadol
Ein Yaakov

1. Moses. Statue by Michelangelo in the Basilica of St. Peter in Chains, Rome.

THE
DIVIDED
KINGDOM

930-722
B.C.E.

Phoe-
nicia

Neighboring

Sovereignties

Dan

Mt. Carmel

Sea of
Galilee

Megiddo

Jordan River

Mediterranean

Sea

Shechem

I S R A E L

Bethel

Jerusalem

Bethlehem

Hebron

Dead Sea

Beersheba

Philis-
tia

J U D A H

Neighboring

Sovereignties

2. Map of Ancient Israel and Judah.

3. Isaiah. Painting by Michelangelo in the Sistine Chapel.

4. Thanksgiving Text in the Dead Sea Scrolls.

5. Philo Judaeus (c. 20 B.C.E. to c. 50 C.E.). Drawing in
a ninth-century manuscript.

6. Page of the Talmud. Isaac Franck Jewish Public
Library, Rockville, Maryland.

7. Solomon ibn Gabirol (1021-1058). Statue, Spain.
Isaac Franck Jewish Public Library.

8. Rashi (Rabbi Solomon ben Isaac, 1040-1105). Drawing. Isaac Franck Jewish Public Library.

רבנו משה ברבי מיימון זל
יד ניסו תתצה ~ כ טבת תתקסח

9. Moses Maimonides (1135-1204). Lithograph by M. Gur-Arieh, Jerusalem, 1935, after a seventeenth-century engraving. Photo Archive of the Beit Hatefutsot, Tel Aviv, Israel.

10. Baruch Spinoza (1632-1677). Engraving. Photo Archive of the Beit Hatefutsot.

11. Israel ben Eliezer (Baal Shem Tov, 1700-1760).
Drawing. Isaac Franck Jewish Public Library.

12. Moses Mendelssohn (1729-1786). Lithograph after a painting by Anton Graff. Photo Archive of the Beit Hatefutsot.

13. Samson Raphael Hirsch. Portrait. Isaac Franck Jewish Public Library.

14. Emma Lazarus (1849-1887). Drawing. Isaac Franck
Jewish Public Library.

15. Sigmund Freud (1856-1939). Portrait. Isaac Franck
Jewish Public Library.

16. Martin Buber (1878-1965). Photograph. Photo Archive of the Beit Hatefutsot.

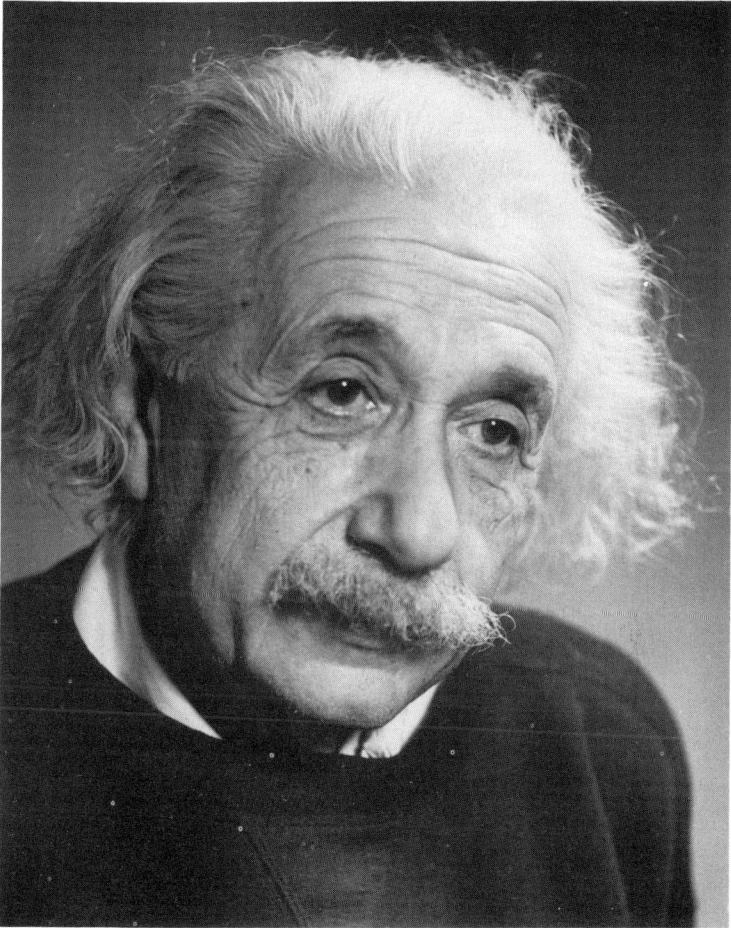

17. Albert Einstein (1879-1955). Photograph, 1955. Fred Stein, *World Celebrities in 90 Photographic Portraits* (New York: Dover Publications, 1988).

18. Abraham Isaac Kook (1865-1935). Drawing.
Benjamin Mazar and others (editors), *The Illustrated History of the Jews* (New York: Harper and Row, 1963).

19. Mordecai M. Kaplan (1881-1983). Photograph by Gedalia Segal. Jewish Theological Seminary, New York.

20. Abraham Joshua Heschel (1907-1972). Photograph
by Lotte Jacobi. *Encyclopaedia Judaica*.

21. Milton Steinberg (1903-1950). Photograph by Dorothy Rolph.

Part Three

NUGGETS OF WISDOM FROM MEDIEVAL JEWISH SAGES

NOTE TO PART THREE

From the vast array of medieval Jewish masterpieces in philosophy, theology, belles-lettres, and other fields of written endeavor, I have culled, for the present purpose, brief excerpts representing selected ideas—which struck me as uniquely appealing or expressed with uncommon elegance—from the works of only seven Jewish writers of the Middle Ages. Therefore, the excerpts included here should *not* be taken as showing either the basic thrust of medieval Jewish reflective thought in general or the basic thrust of what these individual thinkers believed.

I. JACOB AL-KIRKISANI, ABOUT 925

Of the seven sages whose writings are excerpted in Part Three of this volume, Jacob al-Kirkisani is undoubtedly the least famous. Indeed, in the words of Leon Nemoy, of Yale University, al-Kirkisani's "stature as a scholar and thinker has *only recently* been brought to light." Nevertheless, Professor Nemoy wrote of al-Kirkisani that he "may justly be regarded as the greatest Karaite mind of the first half of the tenth century."

Karaism was a Jewish sect whose main tenet was that only the Written Law (the Torah) is valid, and the so-called Oral Law (incorporated in the Talmud) may be disregarded.

Al-Kirkisani, who lived near Baghdad, Iraq, wrote (in Arabic) a commentary on nonlegal portions of the Torah. He opened that commentary with the following words:

164   "Let us begin with an explanation of the meaning of *In the beginning*, since this is the first word in the Law, embracing hidden meanings and abstruse problems which require discussion and thorough investigation, especially on the part of him who undertakes to interpret it in the light of matters rational and philosophical.

"Indeed, some scholars who have attempted to do this without possessing skill in both of these things, that is, the text of Scripture and rational speculation, have imagined that the biblical account of creation and its sequence conflicts with the principles of philosophy and nature.

"This, however, is not so, and he who has armed himself with a true knowledge of both these disciplines knows that each one of them confirms the other; indeed, Scripture is really one of the foundations of philosophy."

On a later page, al-Kirkisani reiterated this theme of the harmony of Scripture and rational reflection. He said:

165   "[As to the fact that] some of our scholars,
       upon hearing an interpretation interspersed
       with matter pertaining to philosophical specu-
       lation, are frightened away from it, . . . this is
       only because of their ignorance and the pov-
       erty of their knowledge. Were the eyes of their
       minds open, they would have learned that
       these things are tools for the understanding of
       Scripture and ladders and bridges toward the
       perception of revealed truth, inasmuch as the
       truth of Scripture and religion can be com-
       prehended only by reason."

Al-Kirkisani recognized that the foregoing broad statements needed to be clarified and supported. Accordingly, he offered the following as a specific example:

166   "Scripture as a whole is to be interpreted lit-
       erally, except where literal interpretation may
       involve something objectionable or imply a
       contradiction. . . . Thus we are compelled to
       say that the verse, *And they saw the God of Israel*
       . . . (Exodus, chapter 24, verse 10), must not
       be understood literally and does not signify
       seeing with one's eye, since it is contrary to
       reason to assume that the Creator may be per-
       ceived with man's senses."

Comment

If the passages just quoted impel any of my readers to
look further into the wisdom of al-Kirkisani, that will
tend to justify and confirm Professor Nemoy's high valuation of al-Kirkisani as a newly rediscovered medieval
thinker.

II. SOLOMON IBN GABIROL, ABOUT 1050

On many pages of this anthology, we shall encounter affirmative doctrines commending piety and righteous conduct and providing guidelines for a life of probity and virtue. The selections presented here, however, from the writings of Solomon ibn Gabirol (of Spain) are negative in tone. They describe the human race as essentially insignificant, and the earth's inhabitants as sinful.

Ibn Gabirol, who is also known as Avicebron, composed a poem entitled *Keter Malkhut* (Kingly Crown), from which two extracts are presented below. In both extracts, his demeaning descriptions of himself (through the use of the word "I") seem intended to apply to everybody.

In the first extract, the phrase "a wind that passeth away and cometh not again" comes from Psalm 78, verse 39.

167   "I am clods and worms, dust of the earth, a vessel full of shame, a dumb stone,

"A fleeting shadow, 'a wind that passeth away and cometh not again,' an adder's venom, . . .

"From nothing I came, and to nothing I go."

In our second extract from ibn Gabirol's *Keter Malkhut*, the emphasis is on human depravity.

168   "I have sinned against Thy law, I have despised Thy commandments,

"I have defiled my heart and my mouth, I have spoken abomination,

"I have done evil, I have done wickedly, I have been presumptuous, I have been violent, I have dealt in falsehood, I have given ill counsel,

"I have lied, I have scoffed, I have murmured, I have blasphemed, I have rebelled, I have trespassed, I have transgressed, I have wronged, I have stiffened my neck,

"I have disdained Thy chastisements, I have
done iniquity,
"I have perverted my paths, I have wan-
dered from my ways,
"I have turned away from Thy commandments, and I have gone astray."

The observant reader may have noticed the similarity
of this confession to the portion of the liturgy for the Day
of Atonement which begins "Ashamnu" (We have in-
curred guilt). Ibn Gabirol was undoubtedly familiar with
the "Ashamnu" text in the service for the Day of Atonement, but it had undergone so many changes, and had
received so many additions over the centuries, that it is
difficult to compare ibn Gabirol's poem with the
"Ashamnu" text of his day.

Comment

The depiction of humanity in the lines of ibn Gabirol's
poem, although consistently gloomy, is redeemed artis-
tically by the richly imaginative language in which the
doleful message is couched. Accordingly, we may turn
away from the above-quoted passages with understanding of the mood which inspired the author when he
wrote them, and we may prepare to learn from other
sages about humanity's equally important potential for a
good and satisfying life.

III. BAHYA IBN PAQUDA, ABOUT 1075

Bahya ibn Paquda, like ibn Gabirol a resident of Spain, presented us with a more positive outlook than his fellow countryman. Bahya's more cheerful wisdom is recorded in his work *Khovot Ha-Levavot* (Duties of the Heart).

The first of the topics on which we shall consider Bahya's teaching is God and the world.

God and the World

1. Bahya concerned himself creatively with a problem which had become prominent in medieval thought, namely, the question, How can we know God? Bahya's view on this question is that we can know God's intention, wisdom, and power *through His creation*. Bahya wrote, on this subject:

169 "If a man were to produce a document with the kind of writing only possible when done with a pen and were to claim that the ink spilled over onto the paper so that the writing emerged of its own accord, . . . we would point out that the thing is impossible.

"Now if this is impossible even with regard to the forms of letters . . . , how can we say of . . . [the whole universe] that it came into being without a Maker's *intention*, the *wisdom* of a Mind, and the *power* of a Powerful Being?"

2. Bahya thus taught that we can confidently know some things about God from experience. He also stated that it is our duty to extend the frontiers of our knowledge of God, especially on the topic of divine-human relations. On our intellectual obligation in this area, he wrote:

170 "[T]he subject *most necessary* to study . . . is the evidence of the divine wisdom shown in all that concerns the human species. . . .

"[I]t is our duty to study the origin of man and his history; his birth, and the composition

and structure of his component parts . . . And
then we must consider . . . his mental qualities
and characteristics, . . . and his relation to the
scheme of Creation."

3. In the same spirit of extending our knowledge of
divine-human relations, and concurrently expressing
gratitude for a special benefit which humans have received from heaven, Bahya said:

171   "The supreme benefit . . . bestowed by the
        Creator on human beings . . . is *Wisdom*."

Moderation as a Guideline

Bahya was among the medieval Jewish sages who favored a way of life which is called "the golden mean." For
example, he urged his readers to choose a middle ground
between solitude on the one hand and excessive socializ-
ing on the other. In that vein, he wrote:

172   "The pure of heart will always love solitude.
        But . . . the temptation to *complete* solitude
        must . . . be guarded against. For the society of
        philosophers, the pious, and of great men is *of
        good advantage*."

Humility

In addition to commending moderation, Bahya was a
staunch advocate of the virtue of humility.

a. To make clear his position on this subject, Bahya
contrasted true humility with pride in general and with
various forms of pride, as follows:

173   "He who has true humility will be free from
        all pride, conceit, self-praise and self-glorifica-
        tion."

b. Bahya also offered separate detailed descriptions of
the person who is humble and the person who is proud.
Regarding the ideally *humble* person, Bahya said:

174   "He who is humble before God should be
        meek and modest in all the affairs of the world;

both in what is seen and in what is secret; in his speech and in his actions; in his bodily activities, and when at rest."

Regarding a basic mistake which the *proud* person makes, Bahya said:

175 "[T]he proud man thinks he is, himself, his own benefactor, and that it is his own wisdom and his own power that . . . [have] gained him the acquisitions of which he is proud."

c. The foregoing pronouncements by Bahya relate primarily to the *attitude* of the humble person and the proud person. Bahya, however, did not leave the matter there. He also described the humble person's *conduct*.

176 "He who is humble before God will not only do good to all men, but he will speak kindly to them and of them; . . . will never relate anything shameful about them; and will forgive them for any shameful things they may say about *him*, even if they are not . . . *worthy* of such treatment."

177 "[T]he meek will . . . never behave oppressively . . . ; but he will *rescue* the oppressed . . . ; and he will teach men to do right, and warn them against evil."

178 "The truly humble man will *mourn* for all the mistakes made by other men, and will not . . . rejoice over them."

d. Bahya depicted humility not only as *morally praiseworthy* but also as *advantageous*, because it produces endurance and contentment.

179 "[W]hen misfortunes come to . . . [the meek], their *endurance* triumphs over their . . . grief."

180 "The humble [person] . . . bears troubles with greater *fortitude* than do the proud."

181   "[T]he humble man assigns no special rank
       to himself, but is content with whatever comes
       to him . . . . And this induces restfulness of
       soul, and minimizes anxiety."

e. Having applauded the virtue of humility in so many
ways, Bahya felt that he should explain to his readers
how to achieve that virtue. He set forth several
techniques for acquiring humility.

182   "Among the aids to the cultivation of . . .
       humility are [1] the contemplation of the great-
       ness of man's obligation to the Creator and [2]
       the thought of how small is his fulfillment of
       his duties. . . . [Additional aids include] con-
       templation of [3] the wonders of the universe
       . . . , [4] the insignificance of man in compari-
       son with . . . this earth and [5] the fact that in
       comparison with the greatness of the Creator
       . . . [man] is nothing."

Role of Reason

Whether contemplating the golden mean, humility, or
other aspects of the good and righteous life, Bahya
placed enormous value on the teachings of Scripture and
tradition, but he also cherished the role of human reason.
In recognition of the weighty role of reason, he wrote:

183   "[T]he duties of the heart involve . . . the
       cultivation of right beliefs based upon *Reason*."

184   "The duties of the heart and mind have . . .
       their roots in human *Reason*, and would be rec-
       ognized as binding even without revelation."

185   "It is the bounden duty of all . . . to search
       out the true meaning of the doctrines they ac-
       cept, and the foundations of these doctrines in
       Reason."

In one of his pronouncements, Bahya declared that the
basis of ethical truth is the *combination* of reason, Scripture, and tradition.

186   "While some . . . duties are only obligatory
       . . . in special circumstances, . . . duties of the
       heart, taught by Reason, Scripture, and Tradi-
       tion, are incumbent upon us continually, . . .
       at every moment."

Reward and Punishment

On the role of reward and punishment (as well as
praise and blame), Bahya made the following momentous declaration:

187   "They who love God will do all that is right,
       without hope of reward; and will forsake all
       that is evil, without fear of punishment. . . .
       And they will be indifferent to the praise and
       blame of men in doing the will of God."

Comment

As we finish our brief savoring of Bahya's wisdom, we
may express our pleasure not only in his insightful thinking but also in his artistic method of expression. On his
enchanting skill in word magic, we may note his own
words:

188   "The tongue is the pen of the heart, and the
       messenger of the distant soul."

IV. RABBI SOLOMON BEN ISAAC (RASHI), ABOUT 1100

Almost since the time when the Bible was produced, Jews have been concerned not only with reading it and cherishing it as Holy Scripture but also with extracting from it every conceivable facet of its message. One of the greatest medieval expounders of the Bible was Rabbi Solomon ben Isaac (France, 1040-1105), who is usually called Rashi, from the initial letters of the words *RA*bbi *SH*lomo ben *I*tzkhak (Solomon son of Isaac).

Rashi is best known as the author of a learned commentary on the Pentateuch and on other books of the Bible. Rashi's commentary on the Pentateuch deeply influenced Christian scholars almost as soon as it appeared. Moreover, it was probably the first Hebrew book to be printed (1475). Thereafter, it began to be translated into other languages (about 1650), and it was itself commented on in more than two hundred studies.

Creation Story

Rashi contended that the opening lines of Genesis should be translated as follows:

189   "At the beginning of the Creation of heaven and earth, when the earth was desolate and void, and there was darkness, *then* God said, Let there be light."

His reason for opposing the conventional translation, "In the beginning God created the heaven and the earth," was that:

190   "[W]herever the word *reshit* [beginning] appears in Scripture, it is in the *construct* [meaning: beginning *of* something. Accordingly, the simple expression 'In the beginning' is *not* what the opening words mean]."

Rashi continued:

191   "Should you insist, however, that . . . the meaning is that in the beginning . . . God

created the heaven and the earth, then you should be surprised to find that the *waters* were really created first, since it is written [*before* God said, 'Let there be light'] that 'The spirit of God hovered over the face of the waters.'"

Regarding the words (appearing later in the first chapter of Genesis) "Let us make man in our image," Rashi's thought was:

192   "He consulted with the angels ['let *us* make,' and he obtained their concurrence, but] the angels did not assist in making man, . . . [for] the subsequent verse . . . states: 'And *God* created.' It does not state: 'And *they* created.'"

Rashi continued commenting on the Biblical account of the stages of the world's creation. When he came to the proposition "And on the seventh day God ended his work" (Genesis, chapter 2, verse 2), he deliberated, "Surely, the work was finished on the *sixth* day (was it not?), and not on the seventh." So he offered an explanation:

193   "What did the world lack [at the end of six days]? Only rest. So when the Sabbath came, *rest* came, and . . . the whole work of Creation was finished."

Story of the Flood

Moving to a later chapter of Genesis, Rashi raised the question of the meaning of the verse "Noah was a just man and perfect in his generations" (Genesis, chapter 6, verse 9). He wrote, on this subject:

194   "Some of the sages interpret the verse in Noah's favor, by observing: . . . 'if he had managed to be righteous in such a *wicked* milieu, how much more righteous would he have been had he lived in an age of *righteous* people!'

> "Others, however, interpret the phrase to his discredit by noting that it implies that Noah was righteous *only* by the standards of his own generation."

According to Genesis, chapter 9, verse 3, God said to Noah after the flood, "Every moving thing that liveth shall be meat for you; even as the green herb have I given you all things." Rashi interpreted God's statement as meaning:

195   "I did not permit Adam to eat meat; only green herbs. But to you (Noah) I have permitted everything."

That is, according to Rashi, Adam and his descendants until Noah's time were vegetarians.

Comment

This small morsel of Rashi's wisdom will have to suffice for our present purpose of indicating that notable Jewish sages of the Middle Ages had things to say which are worth hearing today.

V. RABBI MOSES BEN MAIMON (RAMBAM), ABOUT 1175

Further enlightenment in the effort to understand the Bible was provided, a few generations after Rashi, by Rabbi Moses ben Maimon (Spain, Holy Land, Egypt, 1135-1204), who is called Rambam, from the initial letters of the words *RA*bbi *M*oshe *b*en *M*aimon (Moses son of Maimon). The second "a" in "Rambam" was added to facilitate pronouncing the "b" in "ben" followed by the "M" in "Maimon." By non-Jewish scholars, Rambam is called Maimonides (a name formed by adding the Greek suffix "-ides," meaning "son of," to the name Maimon).

Rambam is the most celebrated Jewish philosopher of the Middle Ages. He contributed not only to Jewish religious doctrine but also to philosophy and theology in general. His arguments for the existence of God were adapted by Saint Thomas Aquinas (1225-1274). Some of Rambam's views on the nature of God were deemed too advanced by rabbis of his own and succeeding generations.

We shall take up Rambam's wisdom under three headings relating to religion (How to Read the Bible, The Nature of God, and Our Knowledge of God) and three headings relating to ethics (Human Freedom, Moderation, and Other Guidelines).

How to Read the Bible

Rambam rejected a literal interpretation of the many references in the Bible to *corporeal* aspects of God, since, as Rambam insisted, God is an incorporeal spirit. On this subject, Rambam wrote, in his *Mishneh Torah* (Repetition of the Law), also called *Yad Khazakah* or *Yad Ha-Khazakah* (Strong Hand):

196   "The Torah speaks in the language of human beings. Hence, all expressions like 'I whet my glittering sword' are *metaphorical*. Has God a sword? Does he slay with a sword? It is a figure of speech; it is . . . figurative."

Besides the *Mishneh Torah*, Rambam's other major work, *The Guide for the Perplexed*, made the same point, namely, that certain passages in the Bible must be interpreted figuratively rather than literally. In the *Guide*, Rambam supported this position by referring to the Aramaic translation of the Bible by Onkelos (a Roman prince who became a Jew), as follows:

197   "Whenever in the Pentateuch the term 'to hear' is applied to God, Onkelos . . . paraphrases it, . . . [saying, for example] that a certain speech *reached* Him, i.e., He *perceived* it [rather than that He heard it]."

In the same spirit, Rambam discussed the word "image" (Hebrew, *tselem*) in the expression "Let us make man in our image" (which Rashi had interpreted, as noted above, from another perspective). Rambam decisively rejected the implication—which might be taken from those words—"that God had the form of a human being." Instead, Rambam said (invoking the philosophical concept of an "essence"),

198   "The word *tselem* . . . signifies . . . that which constitutes the *essence* of a thing, whereby the thing *is what it is*."

That is, according to Rambam, God made human beings as having (to some degree) the same *essence* as God (namely, the essence of being a conscious and intelligent living thing).

The Nature of God

One of the propositions on which Rambam was most insistent is that God does not change. He wrote, in the *Mishneh Torah*:

199   "If God were sometimes angry and [He] sometimes rejoiced, He would be changing. [But we are told by the prophet Malachi, 'I am the Lord, I change not.']."

In *The Guide for the Perplexed,* Rambam carried even further the notion that God does not change. He wrote:

200   "[God is not] a being that is subject [in any way] to the relation of time . . . just as we do not say 'crooked' or 'straight' in reference to taste, [or] 'salted' or 'insipid' in reference to the voice."

That is, we should not say of God that something *was true* of Him once but is not true now, or that something *will become true* of Him later which is not true of Him now.

In some of his writings, Rambam expounded the conventional teachings of Judaism as venerable truths. Nevertheless, he repeatedly warned, in his philosophical works, that we must not speak of God's positive attributes. What we may acknowledge about God, according to Rambam, is God's actions or deeds:

201   "[W]e can only obtain a knowledge of . . . [God] through His works; His works give evidence of His existence, and show . . . what must be attributed to Him."

It is not clear, however, from a reading of Rambam's writings how one may reconcile (1) his teaching that God does not change, and is outside of time, with (2) his teaching that God engages in actions or deeds at particular times.

Our Knowledge of God

In the area of what we can know about God, Rambam was a supporter of what philosophers call the *via negativa;* that is, the view that we can know only *negative* facts about God, such as: God is not this, God is not that. (We have already seen one manifestation of the *via negativa* in Rambam's statement that we may not ascribe positive attributes to God.) Rambam wrote, on this subject:

202   "[T]hat which lies in our power to know about God, we can know only by means of

negation. . . . But through negation we can
never know . . . the true nature of that . . .
[about] which the negation is made.

"The only form of comprehension of God we
can have is to realize how futile it is to try to
comprehend Him."

The same position was also stated by Rambam in other
language, as follows:

203   "[We must] approach the knowledge of God
       . . . by such researches and studies as would
       show us the *inapplicability* of what is *inadmissi-
       ble* as regards the Creator."

In defending his support of the *via negativa*, Rambam
felt the necessity of commenting on the many *affirmative*
statements about God which appear in the liturgy. As an
observant Jew, he joined in the communal chanting of
such statements. As a philosopher, however, he
staunchly rejected such ideas, arguing:

204   "There is no necessity . . . to use positive at-
       tributes of God with the view of magnifying
       Him."

I pause in this march through Rambam's unconven-
tional views to point out that he was thoroughly aware of
the drastic nature of his theological perspective. Indeed,
in some passages of his writings, he said that these radi-
cal views should *not* be indiscriminately purveyed to the
general public. For example:

205   "This [standpoint, that is, the *via negativa*] is
       not for publication to the masses."

We turn now from Rambam's views on religion (the
Bible, the nature of God, and our knowledge of God) to
his views on aspects of human conduct (freedom, moderation as an ideal, and other ideals or guidelines for a
good and righteous life).

Human Freedom

Rambam discussed human freedom in *The Guide for the Perplexed* and in the *Mishneh Torah*. In the *Guide*, he simply asserted that human beings are endowed with freedom of choice:

206   "Free will is granted to every man. If he wish
        to direct himself to the good way and become
        righteous, the will to do so is in his hand; and if
        he wish to direct himself to the bad way and be-
        come wicked, the will to do so is in his hand."

In the *Mishneh Torah*, Rambam struggled with the problem of harmonizing God's sovereignty with human freedom, and he concluded:

207   "[T]he answer to this . . . [riddle] is 'longer
        than the earth and wider than the sea' [quoted
        from the Book of Job]. It is not given to humans
        to understand this matter fully."

Moderation as a Guideline

On an earlier page, we noted Bahya ibn Paquda's admiration of the golden mean, or moderation, as an ideal of life. Rambam also favored following the golden mean in general, but he mentioned particular situations in which some other guideline should be followed instead. Let us begin by examining two passages in Rambam's writings in which he praised the golden mean. Both of them occur in the *Mishneh Torah*.

208   "[A] person should be neither hot-tempered
        and easily provoked to anger, nor should he be
        like a corpse that has no feeling."

209   "One should not be addicted to jesting and
        mockery; nor should one be sad and mournful
        . . . . One should not be greedy, hastening
        after riches, nor lazy and idle."

In two other passages, Rambam warned *against* a too-rigid adherence to the golden mean. Of these, one passage appears in the *Mishneh Torah*, as follows:

210   "There are some dispositions in regard to
       which it is forbidden merely to keep to the mid-
       dle path. . . . Such a disposition is pride. . . .
       The right way in this regard is . . . to be hum-
       ble-minded and lowly of spirit to the utmost."

The other such passage, rejecting universal adherence
to the golden mean, appears in Rambam's commentary
on the tractate "Abot" in the Mishnah. In that commentary, Rambam wrote:

211   "[I]f the interval between haughtiness and
       complete lowliness be divided into sixty-four
       parts, one should stand on the sixty-third
       step."

Additional Guidelines
Which Rambam Favored

In three passages of the *Mishneh Torah*, Rambam emphasized the importance of care in speaking.

212   "A wise man . . . [i]f he finds that his words
       are helpful and heeded, . . . speaks; other-
       wise, he keeps silent."

213   "A wise man . . . dwells on the *merits* of his
       fellow man, without ever disparaging him."

214   "One must not make a habit of using flatter-
       ing speech."

In various places in his writings, Rambam offered
memorable pronouncements regarding education and
scholarship. Two such pronouncements from the *Mishneh Torah* follow:

215   "There is no honor higher than that which is
       due to the teacher."

216   "A man . . . should eat and drink in the com-
       pany of scholars."

In his *Guide*, Rambam offered the following advice on
educational priorities:

217   "[H]e who wishes to attain to human perfec-
tion must . . . first study Logic."

Here is what Rambam had to say about the virtue of
forgiveness:

218   "Anyone who hastens to forgive deserves
praise."

On the importance of acting virtuously at all times,
Rambam wrote, in the *Mishneh Torah*:

219   "Every man should regard himself during
the whole year as though he were half innocent
and half guilty, and also to regard the whole
world in that light; so that were he to commit
but one sin more, he would incline himself and
the entire world towards the scale of guilt, and
cause its destruction.

"On the other hand, were he to perform one
commandment, he would incline himself and
the entire world towards the scale of merit, and
bring salvation and deliverance to himself as
well as to others."

Comment

In surveying the priceless wisdom of medieval Jewish
sages, we have thus far explored selected themes in the
thinking of five such sages, namely:

Jacob al-Kirkisani
Solomon ibn Gabirol
Bahya ibn Paquda
Rabbi Solomon ben Isaac (Rashi) and
Moses ben Maimon (Rambam)

The remaining sages whose writings we are to savor in
this survey are:

Rabbi Levi ben Gershom and
Joseph Albo

VI. RABBI LEVI BEN GERSHOM (GERSONIDES), ABOUT 1325

As we noted on an earlier page, Rambam was so puzzled by the problem of harmonizing God's providence with human freedom that he said the solution is "longer than the earth and wider than the sea."

The problem which Rambam described as enormously difficult has continued to exercise the mental ingenuity of philosophical thinkers to the present day. Rabbi Levi ben Gershom (France, 1288-1344) was one of those who undertook to study the problem. This thinker is also known as Ralbag (from the elements of his name), or Gersonides (son of Gershom or Gerson), or Leo Hebraeus.

As a result of his deliberations, Gersonides wrote, in his book *Sefer Milkhamot Adonai* (Book of Wars of the Lord):

220 "God foreknows . . . only the *possibilities* open to a man in his freedom, not the particular decisions he will make."

Comment

It should be noted, in this connection, that (just as Rambam was condemned by traditionalists) Gersonides' enemies criticized *him* by saying that his book should be called not *Book of Wars of the Lord* but *Book of Wars Against the Lord*.

The title *Book of Wars of the Lord* was not original with Gersonides. It had been used previously by a Karaite writer, Salmon ben Jeroham (died in Syria about 950), whose title, when translated from Arabic into Hebrew, was *Sefer Milkhamot Ha-Shem* (Book of Wars of the Holy Name).

VII. JOSEPH ALBO, ABOUT 1425

While Gersonides was concerned with the puzzle of human freedom, Joseph Albo (Spain, fifteenth century) discussed another philosophical perplexity—relating to God's omnipotence. This perplexity is sometimes expressed in the form of the question, Can God make a stone so heavy that even *He* cannot lift it?

Albo's solution of the puzzle, presented in his book *Sefer Ha-Ikkarim* (Book of Principles), was: It is meaningless to assert that God either can or cannot do something which involves a self-contradiction. Albo said:

221   "[W]e cannot imagine that even God can make a part equal to the whole; or a diagonal of a square equal to one of its sides; or . . . two contradictory propositions true at the same time."

Comment

I hope that readers of Part Three will have found the wisdom of the sages quoted herein as worthy of note—and worthy of reflection.

Part Four, following an appendix to Part Three, will cover modern Jewish wisdom.

Appendix to Part Three

MAJOR WRITINGS OF THE SEVEN AUTHORS

1. Jacob al-Kirkisani (about 925)

a. *Book of Lights and Watch-Towers* (in Arabic), a code of Karaite law, including essays on the application of reason to theology, methods of interpreting the Torah, liturgy for the Sabbath, etc.

b. *Book of Gardens and Parks* (in Arabic), a commentary on the nonlegal parts of the Torah.

2. Solomon ibn Gabirol (about 1050)

a. *Mekor Khayyim* (Source of Life), a philosophical dialogue between a teacher and a pupil. Ibn Gabirol wrote this work in Arabic, but the Arabic text is no longer extant. For a long time, the work was ignored by Jewish philosophers because its orientation was religiously neutral. The *Encyclopaedia Judaica* describes the work as follows:

> "[I]t expounds a . . . philosophic-religious system wholly lacking in specifically Jewish content and terminology. The author does not . . . quote the Bible, Talmud, or Midrash."

After ibn Gabirol's death, his dialogue was translated into Latin under the title *Fons Vitae*. Ibn Gabirol's name was Latinized as Avicebron, and "he was generally regarded [as] a Muslim, although some Christians thought he was a Christian" (*Encyclopaedia Judaica*). Saint Thomas Aquinas and other Christian medieval philosophers expressed their agreement or disagreement with his views.

Eventually, a Hebrew translation of the dialogue was made, and in the nineteenth century Avicebron was definitely identified as a Jew.

b. *Tikkun Middot Ha-Nefesh* (Improvement of the Moral Qualities), a treatise on ethics. This work also was written in Arabic, but a Hebrew version was prepared by the famous translator Judah ibn Tibbon.

c. *Keter Malkhut* (Kingly Crown), a book of poems.

3. Bahya ibn Paquda (about 1075)

Khavot Ha-Levavot (Duties of the Heart). This work was written in Arabic. It was translated into Hebrew by Judah ibn Tibbon. As a result of its popularity, it was further translated into Italian, Portuguese, Spanish, Yiddish, and (more recently) English, French, and German.

4. Rabbi Solomon ben Isaac (Rashi, about 1100)

a. Commentaries on the Pentateuch, on other books of the Bible, and on the Talmud. Rashi's commentary on the Talmud is printed in the margins in the standard printed editions of the Talmud.

b. Responsa (replies to queries on law and ritual).

5. Rabbi Moses ben Maimon (Rambam, about 1175)

a. *Mishneh Torah* (Repetition of the Torah), also called *Yad Khazakah* or *Yad Ha-Khazakah* (Strong Hand), a compendium of the Oral Law (Talmud and Midrash), organized according to Rambam's own classification of topics. When dealing with different opinions expressed in the Talmud, Rambam takes one position, which he lists as the right one.

b. *Moreh Nebukhim* (Guide for the Perplexed), written in Arabic. This work was translated into Hebrew by Samuel ibn Tibbon.

c. *Siraj* (Commentary on the Mishnah). Portions of this work were issued separately as individual documents, including:

i. Rambam's commentary on the tractate "Abot" (Fathers), and

ii. *Shemonah Perakim* (Eight Chapters), which is an *introduction* to Rambam's commentary on "Abot."

d. *Sefer Ha-Mitzvot* (Book on the Commandments), in which Rambam gave his own listing of the 613 injunctions laid down in the Torah.

e. *Iggeret Teiman* (Epistle to Yemen), on the importance of remaining steadfast in adherence to Judaism despite threats of forced conversion to Islam.

f. *Millot Higgayon* (Treatise on Logic), written while Rambam was a youth.

g. Responsa (replies to queries on law and ritual).

h. Medical works, dealing with asthma, hemorrhoids, poisons, preservation of youth, sexual intercourse, and other subjects.

6. Rabbi Levi ben Gershom (Gersonides, about 1325)

a. *Sefer Milkhamot Adonai* (Book of Wars of the Lord), in which Gersonides discussed numerous philosophical and religious questions by first quoting the opinions of predecessors such as Aristotle, Avicenna, Averroes, and Rambam, and then expounding his own position.

b. Commentaries on selected books of the Bible.

c. Commentaries on Aristotle, Euclid, and Averroes.

7. Joseph Albo (about 1425)

Sefer Ha-Ikkarim (Book of Principles), in which, for example, Albo distinguished three kinds of law, namely, natural, conventional, and divine.

Part Four

NUGGETS OF WISDOM FROM
MODERN JEWISH THINKERS

NOTE TO PART FOUR

When I decided to carry forward into the modern period my quest for Jewish wisdom elegantly stated, I was motivated to persevere in my search by a question asked (in Hebrew) by the eighteenth-century poet and scholar Moses Hayyim Luzzatto. His question—which powerfully invigorated my project—was: "How shall a man obtain wisdom *if he does not look for it?*"

In asking that trenchant question, Luzzatto used the word "man" (Hebrew, *ha-'adam*) to refer to human beings in general. This leads me to express the hope that my readers, if they decry the use of "man" to refer to all of humankind, will be understanding when they encounter instances of that usage throughout Part Four.

In making the selections for Part Four, I was faced with the need to decide which purveyors of wisdom were to be included in the category of "modern Jewish thinkers." With regard to *modernness*, I chose the year 1500 as the earliest date. The other half of the question (Who is a *Jewish* thinker?), I have answered on the basis of the specification which was invented by Isaac Franck, of Washington, D.C., when he had to say whether Spinoza was not only a Jew and a thinker but specifically a *Jewish thinker*. In an article published in 1979, Franck said that a Jewish thinker is one:

> 1. Whose outlook arose, in considerable part, from the matrix of Jewish thought and experience, and

> 2. Whose ideas, or many of them, can be seen to be contributions to the later development and advancement of Jewish thought.

On that basis, Franck included Spinoza among Jewish thinkers.

On the same basis, for the purpose of the present anthology, I have, for example, included Albert Einstein among modern Jewish thinkers. It is true that Einstein's religious ideas differed materially from conventional Jewish thinking, but his declarations on religion *arose* in a quasi-Jewish matrix, and they *contributed* to the later development and advancement of Jewish thinking.

Also on that basis, I have excluded, among others, Henri Bergson from the category of modern Jewish thinkers. Bergson, I acknowledge, affirmed his Jewishness by rejecting the French authorities' offer to exclude him from the Nazi edicts against the Jews. His philosophy, however, *did not arise* in a Jewish matrix and *did not contribute* to the later development and advancement of Jewish thinking.

I
HOW DOES THE WORLD OPERATE?

Modern Jewish thinkers have exercised their wisdom in coping with the following basic aspects of the question, How does the world operate?

1. Does everything that happens happen *by necessity?*
2. Is there a basic *mystery* about how the world operates?
3. Is everything in the world *sacred?*

1. Does Everything That Happens Happen *by Necessity?*

Spinoza's View. Baruch (Latinized as Benedict) Spinoza (the Netherlands, 1632-1677) affirmed that the world operates on the basis of necessity. In his book *Ethics Proved in Geometric Order*, he stated:

222   "[A]ll things in nature proceed eternally from a certain necessity."

From that position, and with the additional idea that cosmic necessity is the same as the *decree of God*, Spinoza reached the following conclusion regarding the vicissitudes of human life:

223   "[W]e should expect and bear both faces of fortune with an equal mind; for all things follow by the eternal decree of God."

Spinoza also concluded, on the basis of the necessity of things, that we should not take a negative view of our encounter with reality:

224   "He who . . . knows that all things follow from the necessity of divine nature . . . will find nothing . . . worthy of hatred . . . or contempt."

In his essay entitled *A Theologico-Political Treatise*, Spinoza drew still another conclusion from his doctrine of cosmic necessity, namely, a repudiation of *miracles*. Of his two striking pronouncements in which he rejected the occurrence of miracles, the first one was:

225   "[A]ny event happening . . . which con-
       travened nature's universal laws would neces-
       sarily also contravene the Divine decree, na-
       ture, and understanding."

His second dictum opposing belief in miracles was:

226   "God's nature and existence, and con-
       sequently His providence, cannot be known
       from miracles; . . . they can . . . be much better
       perceived from the fixed and immutable order
       of nature."

Luzzatto's View. About a century after Spinoza's time, Moses Hayyim Luzzatto (Italy and the Netherlands, 1707-1746) took a position opposed to Spinoza's necessitarianism. Luzzatto declared, in a work entitled *Derekh Ha-Shem* (The Way of God):

227   "There is absolutely *nothing* that He [God]
       must necessarily do."

As a purely biographical diversion (and apart from philosophical thinking), it may be of interest to note that Spinoza worked as a lens-grinder in Amsterdam, and Luzzatto worked as a gem-cutter in the same city.

Einstein's View. In the twentieth century, Albert Einstein (Germany, Switzerland, Czechoslovakia, United States, 1879-1955) reverted to Spinoza's necessitarianism. Rejecting the "uncertainty principle" with reference to subatomic particles, Einstein wrote as follows to the physicist Max Born:

228   "*You* believe in the dice-playing God, and *I*
       in the perfect rule of law within a world of . . .
       objective reality."

Many anecdotes have circulated regarding Einstein's rejection of a dice-playing God. According to one such story, Einstein was said to have spoken as if God were his uncle. According to another, Einstein was said to have spoken as if *he* were *God's* uncle. In still another tale, a colleague said to Einstein, "Stop telling God what to do."

Comment. Whether everything that happens does so according to necessity, it is difficult to say. In one sense, *after* something has happened, it is often possible to offer a full scientific explanation of why it happened the way it happened. On the other hand, *before* something happens, it is often impossible to predict what will actually happen—partly because of the element of human freedom (which Einstein, however, rejected). We therefore leave this issue open for further clarification by future philosophers.

2. Is There a Basic *Mystery* About How the World Operates?

Einstein's View. Einstein, although he firmly advocated necessitarianism, nevertheless acknowledged that there is an element of deep mystery about how the world operates. He also gloried in the element of mystery, and he associated it with religion. He wrote:

229 "The most beautiful and deepest experience a man can have is the sense of the mysterious. It is the underlying principle of religion."

He added:

230 "The fairest thing we can experience is the mysterious. . . . He who knows it not . . . is . . . a snuffed-out candle."

Referring to the religious scientist, Einstein stated:

231 "His religious feeling takes the form of rapturous amazement at the harmony of natural law which reveals an intelligence of such superiority that, compared with it, all the systematic thinking and acting of human beings is an utterly insignificant reflection."

Edman's View. Irwin Edman (United States, 1896-1954) wrote in prose and verse on the philosophy of religion and on other topics. Born a Jew, he became an unbeliever, but he concluded that, even for a modern mind, reason is not enough, and a *mysterious sense of eternity* seems to prevail:

232 "I am too lessoned in the changeless law . . .
　　　To . . . [view experience] with trembling awe, . . .
　　　Yet while thus Reason routs these dreams and fears,
　　　Eternity keeps thundering in my ears."

Comment. Not only believers but also nonbelievers agree that there is an element of mysteriousness which pervades the entire cosmos. We can therefore reasonably accept this doctrine as warrantedly credible.

3. Is Everything in the World *Sacred*?

Related to the question whether mystery is apparent everywhere is the question whether sacredness or holiness is also to be found everywhere.

Buber's View. Martin Buber (Austria, Germany, and Palestine/Israel, 1878-1965) cited with approval a Hasidic master who, on the question whether everything is sacred, began his teaching by referring to God's having instructed Moses to remove his shoes at the burning bush because the ground was holy. The Hasidic master then said (according to Buber):

233　　"[Any] place on which you happen to be
　　　standing . . . is holy ground. For there is no
　　　rung of being on which we cannot find the ho-
　　　liness of God."

Comment. It can be uplifting and inspirational to regard everything in the world as sacred; and there seem to be no overwhelming considerations against it. Therefore, we may count this hypothesis as adequately well founded.

II

WHAT CAN BE SAID ABOUT THE GOD WHO GOVERNS THE WAY THE WORLD OPERATES?

The questions into which the topic of this chapter breaks down are as follows:

1. Does God really *exist*?
2. Can we *know* God?
3. How may God be most credibly *described*?
4. What are the basic *relations* between God and human beings?

1. Does God Really *Exist*?

Some philosophers, especially in earlier periods, have thought that one could *prove* the existence of God. Nowadays, however, most of those who have studied this topic lean toward the more moderate view that one can give *plausible reasons*, and even *persuasive reasons*, for believing in God's existence, but one cannot provide a conclusive logical proof of it consisting of immaculate reasoning from unexceptionable premises.

The first view to be set forth here on this subject is an effort by Spinoza early in the modern period to prove the existence of God through what he deemed to be correct reasoning from starting points which are universally accepted.

Spinoza's View. Spinoza's reasoning consisted of a set of *definitions*, a *premise* based on what we all experience, and what he considered to be inevitable *conclusions* from the definitions and the premise, as follows:

234

Definition 1

"God I understand to be a being absolutely infinite."

Definition 2

Existence is *having power*. "Inability to exist is want of power, and, on the other hand, ability to exist is power."

Premise
The ordinary things of everyday experience
exist and *have power*.

Preliminary conclusion 1
If everyday things existed and God did not
exist, then "finite things . . . [would be] more
powerful than a being absolutely infinite; and
this . . . is absurd."

Preliminary conclusion 2
"Therefore, either nothing exists, or a being
absolutely infinite necessarily exists."

Decisive conclusion
But, since everyday things do exist (for
example, I exist), therefore "a being absolutely
infinite, that is, . . . God, necessarily exists."

Spinoza's proof, as just outlined, may be commented
on in various ways. One possible objection to the proof is
the idea that defining God simply as an absolutely infinite being does not include in the concept of God all that
we really want to refer to when we think about God. A
being which is merely absolutely infinite could be the
physical universe (if the physical universe is indeed infinite, contrary to what some cosmologists say).

In any case, I turn now to an example of the procedure
which I referred to above as arguing for the existence of
God by giving *plausible reasons* therefor.

Steinberg's View. Milton Steinberg (United States,
1903-1950), in his book *Anatomy of Faith*, which was published ten years after his death, presented a number of
intriguing reasons for believing in God's existence. He
wrote:

235   "To believe in God maturely . . . is to believe
         that reality did not just 'happen,' that it is no
         accident, no pointless interplay of matter and
         energy. It is to insist rather that things, includ-
         ing man's life, make sense, that they add up to

something. It is to hold that the universe, physical and moral, is a cosmos, not an anarchy."

He also asserted:

236 "God is the only tenable explanation for the universe, [especially for the following facts about the universe]:

1. "[T]he universe is *one*, an organic unity, subject everywhere to the same law, knitted together with interdependence. . . .

2. "[I]t is *dynamic*, pulsating with energy, movement, life.

3. "It is *creative*, forever calling new things into being, from stars and solar systems to new breeds of animals, new ideas in the minds of men, new pictures on the artist's canvas.

4. "It is *rational* in the sense that everything in it behaves according to law . . . not only of chemistry, physics, and biology but of psychology and the moral order as well. . . .

5. "The universe, furthermore, is *purposive;* at least . . . in some of its phases. An insect laying its eggs in a place where the larvae yet to be born will be assured of food . . ., a spider weaving its web, a bird building a nest, an engineer designing a bridge, . . . a prophet blueprinting a perfected mankind—all these are instances, . . . conscious or instinctual, of planning ahead.

6. "The universe . . . contains *consciousness.*"

Steinberg concluded as follows:

237 ". . . For such a universe, the religious theory is by far the best 'fit.'

"... [T]he God-faith ... leaves less unexplained than does its alternative. If the be-
liever has his troubles with evil, the atheist has
more and graver difficulties to contend with.
Reality stumps him altogether, leaving him
baffled not by one consideration but by many,
from the existence of natural law through the
instinctive cunning of the insect to the brain of
the genius and the heart of the prophet.

"This then is the intellectual reason for believing in God: that, though this belief is not
free of difficulties, it stands out, head and
shoulders, as the best answer to the riddle of
the universe."

Comment. Steinberg's view, in favor of belief in God,
is not something that can be either definitely *established* or
refuted. One must take from it what one can acceptably
find in it.

2. Can We *Know* God?

Suppose that Steinberg's support for believing in
God's existence appeals to a thinking individual as both
attractive and credible. That individual may next reasonably ask, Can I *know* God?

Spinoza's View. According to Spinoza, not only can
we know God—intuitively—but such knowledge is a
priceless boon. He said:

238   "The greatest good of the mind is the knowl-
       edge of God, and the greatest virtue of the
       mind is to know God."

Also:

239   "[B]lessedness ... arises from the intuitive
       knowledge of God."

In evaluating these propositions, however, we must bear
in mind that they apply to Spinoza's *conception* of God
(that God is identical with Nature).

Rosenzweig's View. A somewhat different notion about knowing God is found in the writings of Franz Rosenzweig (Germany, 1886-1929). In his influential book *The Star of Redemption*, Rosenzweig propounded an ambivalent view, partly negative and partly positive, on our ability to know God. He wrote:

240   "Of God we know nothing. But this igno-
        rance . . . is the beginning of our *knowledge* of
        him."

Baumgardt's View. A similar view, also partly nega-tive and partly positive, was put forward by David Baumgardt (Germany, United States, 1890-1963), who was Consultant in Philosophy at the Library of Congress. Baumgardt wrote:

241   "[T]he ineffable, which is the object of reli-
        gion, cannot be *grasped* in the rational,
        philosophical statement. It can only be *inti-
        mated*—and only by the artist and the poet."

Comment. It seems to be agreed that, if we know God at all, we know Him primarily by intuition and intima-tion. That we know God *directly* is held only by those who have had a personal mystical experience; and those who have had such an experience (including some Hasidic masters) are unable to communicate it in words.

3. How May God Be Most Credibly *Described*?

Among the questions about the nature of God which modern Jewish thinkers have tried to explain or discuss are:

    a. Is God everywhere?
    b. What can be said about God's nature in
       general?

Is God Everywhere?

Solis-Cohen's View. On the question whether God is everywhere, Solomon Solis-Cohen (United States, 1857-1948), a physician and a poet, wrote:

242 "O Lord, where shall I find Thee?
         Hid is Thy lofty place;
      And where shall I *not* find Thee,
         Whose glory fills all Space? . . .

      Who saith he hath not seen Thee,
         The heavens refute his word;
      Their hosts declare Thy glory,
         Though never voice be heard."

That God not only is everywhere but specifically *dwells within us*, is a further thought which Solis-Cohen expressed:

243   "Dare mortal think such wonder?
             And yet, believe I must,
          That God, the Uncreated,
             Dwells in this frame of dust."

View of a Rabbi of Kotsk. During the period in which Solomon Solis-Cohen lived in the United States, the city of Kotsk, in Poland, produced several prominent Hasidic rabbis. One of them, who is usually identified as "the Rabbi of Kotsk," said, as to whether God is everywhere: Yes, with qualifications. The Rabbi of Kotsk declared:

244   "God dwells wherever man lets Him in."

Reconstructionist View. Another view on whether God is everywhere (namely, that God is especially there where humans live gloriously) is found in the Reconstructionist Prayer Book:

245 "Behold I find Thee
      Wherever the mind is free to follow its own bent,
             . . .
      Wherever men struggle for freedom and right,

Wherever the scientist toils to unbare the secrets of
    nature,
Wherever the poet strings pearls of beauty in lyric
    lines,
Wherever glorious deeds are done."

Comment. Of the two views cited—that God is
everywhere and that God dwells within us if we let Him
in—each seems to contain an important truth.

What Can Be Said About God's Nature in General?

Spinoza's View. According to Spinoza, God is identical with Nature, but Nature includes *thought*. Therefore,
Spinoza said,

246   "God is a *thinking* thing."

Cohen's View. From another angle, Hermann Cohen
(Germany, 1842-1918), professor of philosophy at Mar-
burg University, commented on the nature of God by
saying that God is all-powerful in *most* respects but not in
all respects, for:

247   "Even God's omnipotence is delimited by
       mathematical and logical reason."

Cohen's idea that God is not all-powerful is a theme that
has been influential in modern theological thought.

Kaplan's View. Mordecai Kaplan (Lithuania, United
States, Israel, 1881-1983) offered further provocative
hypotheses regarding God's nature. Specifically, with
reference to the *advance* in human conceptions of God
from a primitive stage to a more sophisticated stage, Kaplan said:

248   "[T]he God-idea progressed from a percep-
       tual image to . . . one which identifies God as
       the sum of all those factors and relationships in
       the universe that make for unity, creativity,
       and worthwhileness in human life."

Kaplan elaborated on this point as follows:

249   "To think of God as a person, with mental
       processes similar to our own, is . . . unsatisfac-
       tory. Yet, if we do *not* think of God in such
       terms, we tend to think of him as analogous
       with some material object or mechanical force,
       which is even less satisfactory.

       "[Furthermore, to] ascribe *consciousness* or
       purpose to God, in the same sense as when we
       apply them to human beings, is absurd. It is
       like ascribing to a multi-millionaire the fact that
       he can afford to buy a newspaper.

Einstein's View. Einstein looked upon God as an "illimitable superior spirit." Einstein's words about the nature of God are:

250   "My religion consists of a humble admira-
       tion of the illimitable superior spirit who re-
       veals himself in the slight details we are able to
       perceive with our frail and feeble mind."

Soloveitchik's View. Rabbi Joseph B. Soloveitchik
(Russia, United States, 1903-1993), instead of expatiating
on an *answer* to our question—What can be said about
God's nature in general?—elaborated on the question itself. According to Soloveitchik, the seeker of basic truth
about the ground of being asks:

251   "Who is He who trails me steadily, uninvited
       and unwanted, like an everlasting shadow,
       and vanishes into the recesses of transcen-
       dence the very instant I turn around to con-
       front this numinous, awesome, and mysteri-
       ous 'He'?"

As to where one may *find* an answer to this question,
Soloveitchik observed that the genuinely inquiring mind

252   " . . . looks for the image of God not in
       mathematical formula or the natural . . . law
       but in every beam of light, in every bud and

blossom, in the morning breeze and the stillness of a starlit evening."

Levinas's View. Emmanuel Levinas (Lithuania,
Ukraine, France, born 1906) studied Talmudic texts in
France with the same teacher who inspired Elie Wiesel
with an admiration for rabbinic insights. Levinas holds
that God is not just the creator of the world and the de-
cider of how the world operates, but also the foundation
or ground of *values*, including moral values. Levinas has
written:

253   "God . . . appears . . . 'clothed' in *values* . . .
        [Indeed, the] ultimate experience of the Divine
        . . . *cannot* . . . *but include* the *values* through
        which the Divine shines forth."

Fackenheim's View. Emil Fackenheim (Germany,
Canada, Israel, born 1916), professor of philosophy at
the University of Toronto, asked some pertinent questions about the nature of God and suggested what the
answers should be.

254   "Is God personal or impersonal? To conceive
        Him as personal is anthropomorphic. Is God,
        then, impersonal—a . . . 'Process'? But this is
        physiomorphic . . . [that is, our model of God
        is taken from the processes of nature; and]
        physiomorphism is even *less* adequate than an-
        thropomorphism; for a 'Process' is qualitatively
        less than a man. The upshot is that we can think
        of God only in symbolic terms.

        "[In that context,] Judaism believes in the co-
        workership of God and man, in the covenant
        between God and Israel, and in God's availa-
        bility in prayer; and the . . . relationship im-
        plied in these beliefs can be thought of only in
        quasi-personal terms."

Comment. As to what can be said about God's nature in general, it seems that incisive Jewish thinkers have held that God is a thinking being, that His omnipotence is limited by the strictures of mathematics and logic (He cannot make the sum of seven and five equal to eleven), He is not a person as we are persons but He is more than something impersonal, He is a superior spirit, and we can think of Him only in symbolic terms.

4. What Are the Basic *Relations* Between God and Human Beings?

With regard to the basic relations which prevail between God and human beings, modern Jewish thinkers have made trenchant pronouncements on the following questions in particular:

> a. How should we view our co-presence with God in the universe?
> b. Are we, in some sense, co-partners with God in conducting the affairs of the world?
> c. Why does God allow the innocent to suffer?
> d. What other features of interest are there in the encounter of God with humanity?

HOW SHOULD WE VIEW OUR CO-PRESENCE WITH GOD IN THE UNIVERSE?

Hasidic View. That human beings regrettably fail to notice our co-presence with God, is a complaint made dolefully by Hasidim. One anonymous Hasidic formulation of this complaint is as follows:

255   "Man's great transgression is that at every instant he could turn to [awareness of the presence of] God—and . . . he does not."

Baeck's View. Leo Baeck (Poland, Germany, England, United States, 1873-1956) wrote, on co-presence with God:

256   "In Judaism, faith is . . . the living con-
        sciousness of the Omnipresent, the feeling of
        the closeness of God, of his revelation and
        creativity, which manifest themselves in all
        things.
            ". . . [Such faith involves] the capacity of the
        soul to perceive the permanent in the transi-
        tory, the Secret in the created."

Heschel's View. Abraham Joshua Heschel (Germany,
Poland, England, United States, 1907-1972) asked several rhetorical questions regarding co-presence, and he
then answered the questions with a pair of exclamations.
The questions were:

257   "Are we alone in the wilderness of time,
        alone in the dreadfully marvelous universe, of
        which we are a part and where we feel like
        strangers? Is there a Presence to live by? . . . Is
        there a way of living in the Presence?"

Heschel's exclamations, which were formulated in
reply to these questions, were intended to shame us into
becoming aware of the co-presence of God:

258   "How embarrassing for man to be the
        greatest miracle on earth and not to under-
        stand it! How embarrassing for man to live in
        the shadow of greatness and to ignore it, to be a
        contemporary of God and not to sense it!"

Comment. As to how we should view our co-presence
with God in the universe, the answer offered by these
thinkers is: *With awareness.*

ARE WE IN SOME SENSE CO-PARTNERS
WITH GOD IN CONDUCTING THE
AFFAIRS OF THE UNIVERSE?

Heschel's View. On the question whether we not only
are co-present with God in the universe but *participate* with
Him in governing what happens, I again quote Abraham
Heschel. According to him,

259   "God's dream is . . . to have mankind as a
       partner in the drama of continuous creation."

Heschel also said:

260   "What is man? A being *in travail* with God's
       dreams and designs."

And:

261   "For man, to *be* is to *play a part* in a cosmic
       drama. . . . Am I not both the chisel and the
       marble?"

Comment. Although it may be hard to believe that we
human beings are co-partners with God, it is perhaps
easier to accept that idea when it is expressed as follows:
By our conduct, we in fact help to *make* the universe what
it is.

WHY DOES GOD ALLOW THE
INNOCENT TO SUFFER?

We now need to examine the question, Why does God
sometimes "hide His face" while the innocent and the
righteous suffer? The metaphor of God as "hiding His
face" (*hester panim*) occurs in Deuteronomy, Psalms, and
Isaiah. The same question, with different metaphors, is
also prominent in Job.

Spinoza's View. Spinoza did not regard God as a personal being, characterized by desires and other feelings.
Therefore, on the question of God's attitude toward unjust suffering, Spinoza wrote:

262   "God cannot pass to a higher or a lower per-
       fection: and therefore he is affected with no
       emotion of pleasure or pain. . . . God, to speak
       strictly, loves no one nor hates any one."

In other words, God—according to Spinoza—does not
concern Himself with protecting the good or punishing
the wicked.

View of a Holocaust Victim. Skipping to the twentieth century, we find that, on the wall of a cellar in Cologne where Jews hid from the Nazis, the following graffito was written:

263   "I believe in the sun even when it is not shining.
       I believe in love even when not feeling it.
       I believe in God even when He is silent."

Einstein's View. Einstein's God resembles Spinoza's in some respects. On the relation of God to the suffering of the innocent, the farthest that Einstein would go was to say:

264   "The Lord God is subtle, but malicious he is not."

Heschel's View. Heschel rejected Spinoza's thought that God is lacking in emotion. Heschel said:

265   "Is it more compatible with our conception of the grandeur of God to claim that he is emotionally blind to the misery of man rather than profoundly moved?"

Heschel seemed to hold that God too suffers when the innocent or the righteous suffer on earth, but God's cosmic plan, of which human suffering is a part, is too great a mystery for us to comprehend.

Hertzberg's View. Arthur Hertzberg (Poland, United States, born 1921) considered the thought, which non-believers have expressed, that suffering is meaningless. Hertzberg's response to that position was:

266   "That suffering is not meaningless, though its meaning is often hidden from us, . . . is the response of faith to tragedy."

Wiesel's View. Elie Wiesel (Romania, Germany, France, United States, born 1928), when asked how he reconciled God's goodness with the Holocaust, began by replying:

267   "I do not understand it."

He then took up the matter of faith, which Hertzberg had declared is the proper response to tragedy. Wiesel said that faith is not a *sufficient answer* to the problem, but faith (especially faith in Israel's Covenant with God) is a *necessary part* of the answer:

268   "I . . . do not agree with those who say: . . .
       faith stands above all else. . . . But . . . without
       faith, we could not *survive*. . . . I can protest
       against God *within* the Covenant, but not *out-
       side* it."

He summarized his position as follows:

269   "The moment an *answer* is given, I get suspi-
       cious; as a *question*, I accept it."

Comment. Apparently the modern Jewish mind, in its confrontation with the suffering of the innocent and the righteous, says either:

    (1) that God does not concern Himself with
    the fate of human individuals, or
    (2) that why a benevolent God allows His
    children to suffer unjustly is an unanswerable
    mystery.

WHAT OTHER FEATURES OF INTEREST
ARE THERE IN THE ENCOUNTER OF
GOD WITH HUMANITY?

We now take up two further aspects of God's encounter with human beings, namely, creation and prayer. We shall examine pronouncements by Franz Rosenzweig and Elie Wiesel on creation, and by the Bal Shem Tov, Abraham Kook, Joseph Hertz, Israel Bettan, Morris Adler, Heschel, and Robert Gordis on prayer. These pronouncements are not intended to cover comprehensively the topic of "other features of interest." They do, however, call for inclusion in a summary of memorable cogitations with which modern Jewish thinkers have enriched our fund of wisdom.

Creation

Rosenzweig's View. Franz Rosenzweig, from whose book *The Star of Redemption* we quoted earlier, commented as follows on the reason for the creation of the world:

270   "God had to create . . . [the world] so that it could nestle under the wings of his providence."

Wiesel's View. Elie Wiesel, *himself* a maker of stories, offered the following explanation of why God created humans:

271   "God made man because *he loves stories*."

Prayer

Baal Shem Tov's View. Israel ben Eliezer (Poland, born about 1700, died about 1760) was the founder of Hasidism in eastern Europe. He is known as the Baal Shem Tov (Master of the Good Name), or by the acronym Besht (formed from the initial letters of Baal Shem Tov). His thought regarding prayer is illustrated by his reaction to the following situation:

> A pious but unlettered Jew, wishing to pray, recited the letters of the Hebrew alphabet and said: "Here, God, are your holy letters. Put them into the right words, and arrange the words in the right order." The unlettered Jew then reported to the Baal Shem Tov what he had done.

The Baal Shem Tov replied:

272   "Your prayer . . . opened the gates of heaven."

Kook's View. Abraham Isaac Kook (Latvia, England, Palestine, 1865-1935), who was the first Ashkenazi chief rabbi of Palestine, commented as follows on the significance of prayer:

273   "Prayer does not desire *to change anything* in
       the divine, which is . . . without alteration, but
       to be exalted together with all the changes to
       which the world and the soul are subject."

Hertz's View. Joseph H. Hertz (Slovakia, United
States, South Africa, England, 1872-1946), who was chief
rabbi of the British Commonwealth, declared:

274   "Prayer is . . . the soul's reaction to . . . the
       uncertainties . . . of life."

Bettan's View. A different perspective on prayer was
expressed by Israel Bettan (Lithuania, United States,
1889-1957), namely:

275   "[Prayer is] a direct approach to the throb-
       bing heart of the universe."

Morris Adler's View. Morris Adler (Russia, United
States, 1906-1966), who was killed by a deranged youth
during a Sabbath service in Detroit, reverted to Hertz's
understanding of prayer as "the soul's reaction" to
human limitations. Adler said:

276   "Prayer is a step on which we rise from the
       self we are to the self we wish to be."

Heschel's View. Heschel offered two revealing descriptions of the nature of prayer:

277   "To pray is . . . to retain a sense of the mys-
       tery that animates all beings . . . . Prayer is our
       humble answer to the . . . surprise of living."

Gordis's View. Related to Bettan's thought that prayer
is an approach to the Almighty is what Robert Gordis
(United States, born 1908) said:

278   "[Prayer is a] striving for close contact with
       the Source of our being."

Comment. The foregoing viewpoints regarding creation and prayer are, I think, highly imaginative and illuminating, whether we accept them literally or not.

III
WHAT ARE THE BASIC TRUTHS
ABOUT HUMAN LIFE?

Among the questions about life which have elicited the special attention of Jewish thinkers in the modern era are the following:

> 1. How should we appraise the significance and value of the human individual?
> 2. What are the most reliable guidelines for living a good and satisfying life?

1. How Should We Appraise the Significance and Value of the Human Individual?

Cohen's View. Hermann Cohen, whose thoughts about the nature of God we quoted on an earlier page, provided, as to the value of the human individual, both a historical perspective and a prescriptive mandate.

a. Cohen's *historical perspective* with reference to the human individual was as follows:

279   "It was the prophets who discovered man's
        innate worth."

Historians of human culture have not sufficiently heeded Hermann Cohen's incisive finding on this subject.

b. Cohen's *prescriptive mandate* applicable to human individuals called for implementation by society of the right of self-government. On this point, Cohen belittled Plato's idea that "philosophers should be kings, or kings philosophers." Cohen said:

280   "[M]ust we assume that the sharp division
        . . . [between] those who govern and those
        who are governed . . . is to be perpetuated
        . . .?

        "Should not all . . . participate in their gov-
        ernment, so that all will be rulers as well as
        ruled?"

Lazarus's View. Emma Lazarus (United States, 1849-1887), through one of her poems, made a momentous contribution to our understanding of the significance and value of the human individual. She invigorated the idea that America should recognize the value of oppressed Europeans, including Jews, who were "yearning to breathe free." Her poem, inscribed on the base of the Statue of Liberty, reads:

281   ". . . Give me your tired, your poor,
          Your huddled masses yearning to breathe free,

          The wretched refuse of your teeming shore,
              Send these, the homeless, tempest-
                  tossed, to me;
          I lift my lamp beside the golden door."

Kaplan's View. In more recent views on the value of the individual, we find Mordecai Kaplan pointing out that, in Jewish institutions of learning, equal value is assigned to any intellectually qualified discussant, irrespective of his social status. Kaplan wrote:

282   "No matter how great the prestige of the
          rabbi who was . . . [the] head of the academy,
          he could not silence the arguments of the
          poorest shoemaker or porter who knew the
          law. That was genuine democracy."

Heschel's View. Abraham Heschel (another giant of recent Jewish thought) described, in two impressive propositions, humanity's exalted status in the universe:

283   "Man is a fountain of immense meaning, not
          merely a drop in the ocean of being."

284   "To be human is to intend, to decide, to challenge, not merely to go on, to react, or to be an
          effect."

Hook's View. Sidney Hook (United States, 1902-1989) indicated that one way of placing a high value on human life is to encourage cultural diversity. He wrote:

285   "[The wisest] philosophy of Jewish life is . . .
[one] in which [Jews,] together with their fellow men, . . . encourage a maximum of cultural diversity, both Jewish and non-Jewish."

Wiesel's View. On the extent to which humanity's in-
herently elevated status has advanced over the centuries, Elie Wiesel said:

286   "In medicine, the sciences, nuclear physics,
computer technology, the human race has
made more progress in the past fifty years than
in the previous three thousand. But in
philosophy, literature, poetry, religion, and
morality, there has been very little progress.

    " . . . [F]rom time to time, we see an advance
here and there; but it is . . . maddeningly
slow."

Comment. The significance and value of the human individual have been astutely recognized by outstanding
Jewish thinkers of the modern era.

2. What Are the Most Reliable Guidelines for Living a Good and Satisfying Life?

Modern Jewish thinkers have produced more quotable
ideas on guidelines for living than on any of the other
topics which we have taken up thus far. From the *Ethics*
of Spinoza in the seventeenth century to the reflections
of Elie Wiesel in the twentieth, we find a plethora of insightful maxims on how to live properly.

Seventeenth Century

Spinoza's View. As stated previously, Spinoza lived
from 1632 to 1677. One of the moral ideals that he favored
is that of returning good for evil. He expressed this
guideline as follows:

287   "He who lives under the guidance of reason
endeavours . . . to repay his fellow's hatred,
. . . contempt, etc., with love and nobleness."

"Control your tongue" is another guideline which Spinoza favored, but he praised it only by implication. What he said explicitly about it is that it is exceedingly difficult to follow:

288   "[M]en govern nothing with more difficulty than their tongues, and can moderate their desires more easily than their words."

Following Spinoza's outpouring of valuable maxims in the seventeenth century, we find in the eighteenth century enlightening wisdom on the best way of life in the writings of a rabbi in southern Europe (Italy) and four rabbis in central and eastern Europe.

Eighteenth Century, Italy

Luzzatto's View. Luzzatto, whose wisdom on other topics we have already encountered, turned his attention to several moral topics, including anger. On anger, he wrote:

289   "[When a teacher and a parent] have to reprove, they should do so without anger, and only with a view to correction. . . . [Such anger as they may display] should be more assumed than real."

Luzzatto praised not only the control of anger but also the exercise of humility. On the latter ideal, he said:

290   "[A]ll the wisdom in the world cannot compare with humility."

Luzzatto declared further that we should regularly engage in self-scrutiny:

291   "[A] man . . . should set aside a special time each day for the practice of self-scrutiny."

Eighteenth Century, Lithuania/Germany

Koidanover's View. Zevi Hirsch Koidanover (Lithuania, Germany, died 1712) is another of our Jewish eighteenth-century sources of wisdom. Koidanover favored giving education a high priority:

292   "[I]n every place where children are learning
       from a wise man, in that place dwells the Di-
       vine Presence."

Eighteenth Century, Poland

Baal Shem Tov's View. A guideline favored by the
Baal Shem Tov may be derived from the reply which he
gave to a follower who had asked what he should do
about a wayward son. The Baal Shem Tov replied:

293   "Love him all the more."

In other words, what your wayward son needs in order
to restore him to higher standards is: More love.

Zusya's View. The Hasidic leader Zusya, or Susia (Poland, born during the eighteenth century and died early
in the nineteenth) urged that everyone should follow
two practices which help to make up a good life. The two
practices are:

> (1) daily scrutiny of one's life, on which we
> quoted Luzzato's guideline above, and
> (2) sincere repentance for the sins which
> one observes in oneself as a result of the
> scrutiny.

On Zusya's two practices (self-scrutiny and repentance),
we have, not his own words, but those of a pupil of his,
who wrote about Zusya:

294   "In the course of the day, he wrote every-
       thing he did on a slip of paper. Before going to
       bed in the evening, he fetched it out, read it,
       and wept [repentantly] until the writing was
       blurred with tears."

Eighteenth Century, Ukraine

Nahman's View. Nahman of Bratzlav (Ukraine, Palestine, 1770-1811) was the great-grandson of the Baal Shem
Tov. He emphasized the calm acceptance of whatever
happens to one:

295   "When a man is able to receive abuse smil-
      ingly, he is worthy of becoming a leader."
296   "Bear in mind that life is short, and that with
      every passing day you are nearer to the end.
      How then can you waste your time on petty
      quarrels?"

Nineteenth Century

From the nineteenth century, we may derive valuable
moral guideposts from a Yiddish maxim, a Hasidic teaching, and the writings of Solomon Ganzfried.

Yiddish Maxim. The following rule for righteous living has come down in the form of a Yiddish maxim,
which may have originated in the last century:

297   "A man should be master of his will and
      slave of his conscience."

Hasidic Teaching. Luzzatto, we noted above, praised
humility as a virtue. An anonymous Hasid, who perhaps
was writing in the nineteenth century, commented as
follows on the question, Why does the Torah praise
Moses for his meekness but does not include humility as
a commandment?

298   "If anyone were humble *in order to keep a com-
      mandment*, he would never attain to true humil-
      ity. . . . [One who interprets humility] as a *com-
      mandment*, and keeps it as such, only feeds his
      pride."

Ganzfried's View. In the context of Spinoza's principle of returning good for evil, and of Nahman's praise of
receiving abuse smilingly, Solomon Ganzfried (Hungary, 1804-1886) wrote:

299   "This is . . . the path of the just, that they are
      insulted and do not insult; they hear them-
      selves reviled and answer not."

Ganzfried also made the following recommendation:

300   "Upon seeing a fellow man engaged in his
        work, it is good manners to bless him by say-
        ing: 'May you prosper in your task.'"

Twentieth Century

From Jewish literature of the twentieth century, we
may cull wise sayings on the good life from writers who
were born in Europe or America. The authors are listed
here according to the place where they were born.

Russia

Shestov's View. Albert Camus and D. H. Lawrence
are among those who acknowledged having been influenced by Lev Shestov (Russia, France, 1866-1938). Contrary to the teaching of previous Jewish thinkers who
praised tranquil acceptance of whatever happens to one,
Shestov wrote:

301   "The summit of human experience, say the
        philosophers, is . . . serenity . . . . But in that
        case, the animals should be our ideal, for in the
        matter of imperturbability they leave nothing
        to be desired. Look at a grazing sheep, or a
        cow. *They* do not . . . sigh for what is not."

Austria

Buber's View. Martin Buber (whose thoughts on
sacredness we quoted earlier) considered the matter of
behavioral guidelines in the context of two distinct ways
of life.

        1. The first way, which he called the "I-It"
    way, consists in our experiencing, or relating
    to, things—and even persons—when we view
    them mainly as *means* to the fulfillment of our
    own purposes.
        2. The second way, which he called the "I-
    Thou" way, consists in our seeing the other

(mainly persons) in a manner which reveals to us *what the other is* from his, her, or its point of view.

Among Buber's rhapsodic declarations regarding this contrast are the following:

302   "[W]ithout *It*, man cannot live; but he who lives with *It* alone is not a [whole] man."

303   "Can the servant of Mammon [who is obsessed with possessions] say *Thou* to his money?"

Germany

Heschel's View. Abraham J. Heschel made one point which is similar to Buber's I-It/I-Thou contrast:

304   "[I]n dealings with people, we behave toward them as if they were . . . means . . . for our own selfish ends. How rarely do we face a person as a person! . . . [Yet] the true meaning of existence is experienced in . . . meeting a person face to face."

Heschel also said:

305   "[L]ive in a way compatible with the grandeur and mystery of living."

Einstein's View. The following guideline was provided by Albert Einstein:

306   "[I]t is plain that we exist for our fellow men—in the first place for those upon whose smiles and welfare all our happiness depends, and next for all those unknown to us personally but to whose destinies we are bound by the bond of sympathy."

Romania

Wiesel's View. Elie Wiesel, when asked about forgiveness, replied:

307   "I am not concerned with forgiveness. Con-
        ciliation, yes, but not forgiveness. Perhaps I
        can forgive what they did to me, but nobody
        appointed me to speak for others."

United States

Untermeyer's View. Louis Untermeyer (1885-1977) rejected serenity and contentment (as Shestov had done),
as follows:

308   "Ever insurgent let me be,
            Make me more daring than devout,
        From sleek contentment keep me free,
            And fill me with a buoyant doubt."

Finkelstein's View. Louis Finkelstein (1895-1991),
president emeritus of the Jewish Theological Seminary of
America, wrote as follows about "the art of the good life":

309   "[An important] step will be taken when
        each of us, following in the footsteps of our
        great leaders, sets aside time each day . . . to
        prepare himself to achieve greatness in the art
        which . . . is common to all people—the art of
        the good life."

Comment. Although some of the foregoing guidelines
may seem mutually contradictory (for example: pursue
serenity; do not pursue serenity), nevertheless there
is a large measure of agreement among modern Jewish
thinkers as to how to live a good and satisfying life.

IV
WHAT HAPPENS WHEN WE DIE?

Modena's View. Leone Modena (Italy, 1571-1648) regarded as unlikely the idea that death is the absolutely final end of the human personality. He wrote:

310   "How can we say that the creature who, by dint of his intellect, builds cities and moves mountains, changes the course of rivers, knows the paths of the high heavens, and can recognize his God—that this creature should come in the end to perish entirely like a horse, or a dog, or a fly?"

Spinoza's View. Agreeing with Modena, Spinoza wrote:

311   "The human mind cannot be absolutely destroyed with the human body . . . [T]here is some *part* of it that remains eternal."

Cohen's View. Hermann Cohen, however, was not so sure about this. According to Cohen,

312   "The Jewish mind approaches all questions of the beyond with a certain reticence and discretion."

Shestov's View. Shestov approached the subject not with reticence and discretion but with a sense of humor. He wrote:

313   "In Paradise, everything is permitted except curiosity."

Comment. Modena's and Spinoza's view, that the soul outlives the body, is appealing, but, as Cohen suggests, discretion calls for hesitation in making a firm pronouncement on the subject.

V
WHAT ARE THE BASIC ATTRIBUTES OF JUDAISM?

Eighteenth Century

Mendelssohn's View. Moses Mendelssohn (Germany, 1729-1786) said, in a discussion with a Christian regarding a comparison of Judaism with Christianity:

314   "I do not deny that I see certain human excesses . . . that tarnish the beauty of my religion. But is there any friend of truth who can claim that his religion is completely free of man-made accretions . . .?"

Nineteenth Century

Disraeli's View. Benjamin Disraeli (1804- 1881), before he became British Prime Minister, responded as follows to a tirade directed against him in the House of Commons by Daniel O'Connell:

315   "Yes, I am a Jew, and when the ancestors of the Right Honorable gentleman were brutal savages in an unknown island, mine were priests in the temple of Solomon."

Hirsch's View. Samson Raphael Hirsch (Germany, 1808-1888) composed the following paean to the impact upon us of the cyclical arrival of time periods marked off by the Jewish calendar:

316   "Priests die, monuments decay, temples and altars fall to pieces, but time remains . . ., and every new-born day emerges fresh and vigorous from its bosom. . . . [T]he children of time . . . [such as months in the Hebrew calendar] are able to find you when immersed in the busy mart of life or in the full career of enjoyment, in the lonely stillness of the prison or on the painful bed of sickness . . ."

Gordon's View. Judah Leib Gordon (Russia, 1831-1892) joyously greeted the arrival of the Jewish holiday Simkhat Torah, which celebrates the completion of an annual cycle of the reading of weekly excerpts from the Torah. (The first word of Gordon's poem on the subject, which is here quoted, means: Your health!)

317 "Lehayyim, my brethren, Lehayyim, I say,
  Health, peace, and good fortune I wish you to-day.
  To-day we have ended the Torah once more;
  To-day we begin it anew, as of yore.
  Be thankful and glad, and the Lord extol,
  Who gave us the Law on its parchment scroll."

Twentieth Century, Born in Austria-Hungary

Freud's View. Sigmund Freud (1856-1939) commented as follows on the durability of Judaism:

318   "With an unexplained power of resistance,
  . . . [the Jewish people] has defied misfortune
  and ill-treatment, developed special character-
  traits, and . . . earned the hearty dislike of all
  other peoples."

319   "The preference which throughout two
  thousand years the Jews have given to spiritual
  endeavours has . . . helped to build a dike
  against brutality."

Twentieth Century, German-Born

Cohen's View. Hermann Cohen (who lived the last eighteen years of his life in the twentieth century) expressed the following thought on universalism in Judaism:

320   "God loves the stranger. . . . [Indeed, nations other than Israel] are quite as much His
  precious possessions as is Israel itself."

Regarding the Jewish idea of the Messiah, Cohen said that it refers to an ideal future society rather than to a particular individual:

321   "[The Messiah is] the moral mankind of an
       historical future."

Einstein's View. Einstein declared that "the sanctifica-
tion of life in its all-inclusive sense" is a basic characteristic of Judaism. He continued, along that line:

322   "There remains . . . something *more* in
       the Jewish tradition, . . . namely, a kind of
       drunken joy and surprise at the beauty and in-
       comprehensible sublimity of this world, of
       which man can attain but a faint intimation."

He also said, with admiration:

323   "It is noteworthy that in the commandment
       to keep the Sabbath holy the animals were also
       expressly included."

Kallen's View. Horace M. Kallen (born in Germany in
1882 as the son of a rabbi; teacher of philosophy at Harvard University and elsewhere in the United States; died
1974) compared Hellenism with Judaism in two ways.
First,

324   "The great Hellenic virtues . . . are temper-
       ance and justice, . . . [which] mean the perfect
       use of what is *already possessed*. . . . The great
       Hebraic virtues . . . are faith, hope, and char-
       ity, . . . [which] mean . . . strain for the *unpos-
       sessed*, something off its balance and struggling
       to regain it."

Secondly, where the Greeks thought of tragic suffering
as the unavoidable outcome of ancient crimes, the
Hebrews have contemplated repentance and forgiveness:

325   "For the Greeks, what was from the begin-
       ning shall be to the end. . . . [The great Greek]
       tragedies . . . portray the inexorable working
       of ancestral curses. . . . For the Hebrews, . . .
       [a] 'repentant' man means a 'forgiving' God."

Twentieth Century, American-Born

Adler's View. Cyrus Adler (1863-1940), Secretary of the Smithsonian Institution and a founder of many Jewish religious and secular organizations, wrote:

326   "My people have survived the prehistoric paganism, the Babylonian polytheism, . . ., Hellenism, . . . Romanism; and it will survive . . . the current materialism, holding aloft the traditional Jewish ideals . . . until the world shall become capable of recognizing their worth."

Goldstein's View. Israel Goldstein (born in Philadelphia in 1896, active in Jewish communal affairs, resident of Israel from 1961; died 1986) reiterated Adler's just-quoted confident prediction regarding Judaism. Goldstein stated:

327   "[T]he time will come when . . . every human spirit shall be encouraged to rise to its full stature of humanity and divinity and when human society shall at last be ordered so as to conform with the principles of justice and righteousness first proclaimed at Sinai."

Ozick's View. Cynthia Ozick (born in New York in 1928, author of fiction and nonfiction on Jewish themes) wrote as follows regarding the Sabbath:

328   "Among ancient peoples, all the days of the week were alike, and that, of course, was natural; to the trees and the fish and the molecules of air, all the days are alike; nothing makes a week.

"Sinai made the Sabbath. The Sabbath is a made, invented, created, *given* thing; it is not a natural thing."

She also declared, regarding the devotion of Jews to the Torah:

329   "[F]eeling homeless, we make a home in Torah."

Comment. I hope that my readers have derived spiritual sustenance from the Jewish wisdom of many eras displayed in the four parts of this anthology.

SOURCES OF QUOTATIONS

NOTE: In this list, the number at the beginning of each entry is the quotation number.

Part One. Nuggets of Wisdom
from Jewish Scriptural Writings

1. Genesis, chapter 1, verses 1 and 3.
2. *Ibid.*, chapter 4, verse 13.
3. *Ibid.*, chapter 18, verses 23-32.
4. Exodus, chapter 3, verse 14.
5. *Ibid.*, chapter 15, verse 11.
6. *Ibid.*, chapter 20, verse 3.
7. *Ibid.*, chapter 23, verses 4, 5, and 9.
8. Leviticus, chapter 19, verses 13, 14, 18, and 32; chapter 25, verse 35.
9. Numbers, chapter 5, verses 6-7.
10. *Ibid.*, chapter 6, verses 24-26.
11. *Ibid.*, chapter 12, verse 3.
12. Deuteronomy, chapter 6, verse 1.
13. *Ibid.*, verse 4.
14. *Ibid.*, verses 5-7.
15. Second Book of Samuel, chapter 12, verses 7 and 9.
16. First Book of Kings, chapter 19, verses 11-12.
17. First Book of Chronicles, chapter 29, verse 11.
18. Isaiah, chapter 1, verses 16-17.
19. *Ibid.*, verse 18.
20. *Ibid.*, chapter 2, verses 3-4.
21. *Ibid.*, chapter 5, verse 7.
22. *Ibid.*, verses 11 and 20.
23. *Ibid.*, chapter 6, verses 1-3.
24. *Ibid.*, verse 8.
25. *Ibid.*, chapter 7, verse 14.
26. *Ibid.*, chapter 9, verse 6.
27. *Ibid.*, chapter 11, verses 6 and 9.
28. *Ibid.*, chapter 30, verse 20.
29. *Ibid.*, chapter 35, verses 1 and 10.
30. *Ibid.*, chapter 40, verses 1, 2, and 4.
31. *Ibid.*, chapter 58, verses 4-7.
32. Jeremiah, chapter 6, verse 14.
33. *Ibid.*, chapter 8, verse 22.

34. *Ibid.*, chapter 17, verses 7-8.
35. *Ibid.*, chapter 33, verses 10-11.
36. Hosea, chapter 8, verse 7.
37. Amos, chapter 5, verses 22, 24.
38. Micah, chapter 6, verse 8.
39. Malachi, chapter 4, verse 2.
40. Ruth, chapter 1, verses 16-17.
41. Job, chapter 1, verse 21.
42. *Ibid.*, chapter 3, verse 11.
43. *Ibid.*, verses 17-19.
44. *Ibid.*, chapter 5, verse 7.
45. *Ibid.*, verse 18.
46. *Ibid.*, chapter 28, verses 9-13.
47. *Ibid.*, chapter 31, verse 35.
48. *Ibid.*, chapter 37, verses 6, 16, 18, and 23.
49. *Ibid.*, chapter 38, verses 2-8, 12, 19, 22, 28, 33, and 36; chapter 39, verses 26 and 27.
50. Psalm 1, verses 1-2.
51. Psalm 8, verses 3-5 and 9.
52. Psalm 15, verses 1-2.
53. Psalm 19, verses 1, 7-9, and 14.
54. Psalm 23.
55. Psalm 24, verses 1-4.
56. Psalm 84, verse 10.
57. Psalm 90, verse 4.
58. Psalm 92, verses 1-3.
59. Psalm 107, verses 23-25 and 28-30.
60. Psalm 136, verses 5-9 and 26.
61. Proverbs, chapter 3, verses 13-18.
62. *Ibid.*, chapter 6, verses 6-8.
63. *Ibid.*, verses 16-19.
64. *Ibid.*, chapter 8, verses 22-23, 27, and 32-33.
65. *Ibid.*, chapter 15, verses 1 and 17.
66. *Ibid.*, chapter 16, verse 32.
67. *Ibid.*, chapter 22, verse 6.
68. *Ibid.*, chapter 27, verse 1.
69. *Ibid.*, chapter 30, verses 18-19.
70. *Ibid.*, chapter 31, verses 10-12, 20, 25-26, and 28.
71. Ecclesiastes, chapter 1, verses 2-4, 7, 9, and 17-18.
72. *Ibid.*, chapter 3, verses 1-2, 4, and 6-8.
73. Song of Songs, chapter 1, verse 13; chapter 2, verses 1 and 8.
74. *Ibid.*, chapter 4, verses 1, 3, 5, and 9-11.

75. *Ibid.*, chapter 5, verses 10, 11, 14, and 16.

76. *Ibid.*, chapter 7, verses 1-2 and 6-7.

77. *The Dead Sea Scriptures in English Translation,* edited by Theodore H. Gaster (Garden City, N.Y.: Doubleday & Co., 1956).

78. *Ibid.*, p. 43.

79. *Ibid.*, pp. 43-44.

80. *Ibid.*, p. 45.

81. *Ibid.*, p. 49.

82. *Ibid.*, p. 60.

83. *The Apocrypha, Translated Out of the Greek and Latin Tongues* (London: Oxford University Press; World's Classics, 1942), p. 163.

84. *Ibid.*, pp. 169-170.

85. *Ibid.*, pp. 173-174.

86. *Ibid.*, p. 201.

87. *Ibid.*

88. *Ibid.*, p. 269.

89. James H. Charlesworth (editor), *The Old Testament Pseudepigrapha* (Garden City, N.Y.: Doubleday & Co., two volumes, 1983), vol. 1, pp. 645-646.

90. *Ibid.*, pp. 18-19.

Part Two. Nuggets of Wisdom from Rabbinical and Other Post-Scriptural Discussions

91. *The Living Talmud: The Wisdom of the Fathers and Its Classical Commentaries,* selected and translated by Judah Goldin (New York: The New American Library, 1957), p. 43.

92. *Ibid.*, p. 46.

93. *Ibid.*, p. 50.

94. *Ibid.*, p. 70.

95. *Ibid.*, p. 74.

96. *Ibid.*, p. 75.

97. *Ibid.*, p. 77.

98. *Ibid.*, pp. 80-81.

99. *Ibid.*, p. 86.

100. *Ibid.*, p. 90.

101. *Ibid.*, p. 101.

102. *Ibid.*, p. 115.

103. *Ibid.*, p. 116.

104. *Ibid.*, pp. 120-121.

105. Arthur Hertzberg (editor), *Judaism* (New York: Washington Square Press, 1963), p. 41.

106. *The Living Talmud*, p. 177.

107. *Ibid.*, p. 141.

108. *Ibid.*, p. 157.

109. *Ibid.*, p. 196.

110. *Ibid.*, p. 219.

111. Nahum N. Glatzer (editor), *Hammer on the Rock: A Short Midrash Reader*, translated by Jacob Sloan (New York: Schocken Books, 1948), p. 19.

112. A. Cohen (editor), *Everyman's Talmud* (London: J. M. Dent & Sons, 1932), pp. 105-106.

113. Glatzer, pp. 106-107.

114. *The Talmud With an English Translation, Berakoth*, edited by A. Z. Ehrman (Jerusalem: El-'Am, four volumes, 1982), vol. 1, pp. 109-110.

115. Cohen, p. 7.

116. Glatzer, p. 58.

117. Cohen, p. 11.

118. Jacob B. Agus, *The Vision and the Way, An Interpretation of Jewish Ethics* (New York: Frederick Ungar Publishing Co., 1966), p. 14.

119. Nahum N. Glatzer (editor), *In Time and Eternity: A Jewish Reader*, translated in part by Olga Marx (New York: Schocken Books, 1946), p. 119.

120. Cohen, pp. 20-21.

121. *Ibid.*, 105.

122. *Ibid.*, p. 106.

123. *Ibid.*, p. 5.

124. *Ibid.*, p. 97.

125. Glatzer, *Hammer*, p. 80.

126. *Ibid.*, pp. 43-44.

127. Glatzer, *In Time*, p. 98.

128. Glatzer, *Hammer*, p. 53.

129. Hertzberg, p. 224.

130. Philip Birnbaum (editor), *The New Treasury of Judaism* (New York: Sanhedrin Press, 1957), p. 269.

131. *Ibid.*, p. 274.

132. *Ibid.*, p. 275.

133. *Ibid.*, p. 276.

134. Cohen, p. 84.

135. *The Living Talmud*, p. 74.

136. Glatzer, *Hammer*, p. 21.

137. Cohen, p. 25.

138. *Ibid.*, p. 206.

139. *Ibid.*, p. 4.

140. Samuel Rapaport (editor), *A Treasury of the Midrash* (New York: Ktav Publishing House, 1968), p. 60.

141. Cohen, p. 18.

142. *Ibid.*, p. 41.

143. Hertzberg, p. 15.

144. Samuel Caplan and Harold U. Ribalow (editors), *The Great Jewish Books and Their Influence on History* (New York: Washington Square Press, 1963), p. 65.

145. Cohen, p. 47.

146. *Ibid.*, p. 172.

147. Glatzer, *Hammer*, p. 41.

148. C. G. Montefiore and H. Loewe (editors), *A Rabbinic Anthology* (Cleveland: The World Publishing Co., 1963), p. 316.

149. Cohen, p. 233.

150. *Ibid.*, p. 237.

151. *Ibid.*, p. 111.

152. *Ibid.*, p. 219.

153. Rapaport, p. 211.

154. Cohen, p. 111.

155. Glatzer, *Hammer*, p. 33.

156. *Israel, Land and Nature* (Jerusalem), vol. 15, Winter 1989-1990, p. 100.

157. Rapaport, p. 245.

158. *The Works of Philo Judaeus*, translated by C. D. Yonge (London: Henry G. Bohn, four volumes, 1854-1855), vol. 2, p. 92.

159. *Ibid.*, vol. 1, p. 353.

160. *Ibid.*, p. 349.

161. *Ibid.*, p. 19.

162. *Ibid.*, vol. 3, p. 145.

163. *Ibid.*, pp. 176-177.

**Part Three. Nuggets of Wisdom
from Medieval Jewish Sages**

164. Leon Nemoy (editor), *Karaite Anthology: Excerpts from Early Literature* (New Haven: Yale University Press, 1952), p. 54.

165. *Ibid.*, p. 55.

166. *Ibid.*, p. 60.

167. Solomon ibn Gabirol, *The Kingly Crown*, translated by Bernard Lewis (London: Vallentine, Mitchell, 1961), pp. 53-54.

168. *Ibid.*, pp. 54-55.

169. Bahya ibn Paquda, *Duties of the Heart*, translated by Edwin Collins (London: John Murray, 1905), p. 64.

170. *Ibid.*, p. 39-40.

171. *Ibid.*, p. 15.

172. *Ibid.*, p. 46-47.

173. *Ibid.*, p. 34.

174. *Ibid.*, p. 36.

175. *Ibid.*, p. 37.

176. *Ibid.*, p. 35.

177. *Ibid.*, p. 36.

178. *Ibid.*, p. 33.

179. *Ibid.*, p. 36-37.

180. *Ibid.*, p. 39.

181. *Ibid.*

182. *Ibid.*, p. 34.

183. *Ibid.*, p. 19.

184. *Ibid.*, p. 18.

185. *Ibid.*, p. 22.

186. *Ibid.*, p. 21.

187. *Ibid.*, p. 48.

188. *Ibid.*, p. 40.

189. *Rashi, Commentaries on the Pentateuch*, selected and translated by Chaim Pearl (New York: W. W. Norton and Co., 1970), p. 31.

190. *Ibid.*

191. *Ibid.*, p. 32.

192. *Ibid.*, p. 32-33.

193. *Ibid.*, p. 33.

194. *Ibid.*, p. 34.

195. *Ibid.*, p. 37.

196. Moses Maimonides, *Mishneh Torah (Yad Hazakah)*, edited and translated by Philip Birnbaum (New York: Hebrew Publishing Co., 1985), p. 7.

197. Moses Maimonides, *The Guide for the Perplexed*, translated by M. Friedländer (New York: Dover Publications, reprint of the second edition, 1956), p. 64.

198. *Ibid.*, p. 13.

199. *A Maimonides Reader*, edited by Isadore Twersky (New York: Behrman House, 1972), p. 45.

200. Maimonides, *Guide*, p. 81.

201. *Ibid.*, p. 202.
202. Louis Jacobs, *Jewish Ethics, Philosophy, and Mysticism* (New York: Behrman House, 1969), p. 80.
203. Maimonides, *Guide*, p. 84.
204. *Ibid.*, p. 86.
205. Jacobs, p. 85.
206. Shubert Spero (editor), *The Faith of a Jew: Selections from Rabbi Moses ben Maimon (Rambam)* (New York: Jewish Pocket Books, 1949), p. 28.
207. Jacobs, p. 90.
208. Maimonides, *Mishneh Torah*, p. 11.
209. *Ibid.*, p. 14.
210. *A Maimonides Reader*, p. 54.
211. *Maimonides' Commentary on Pirkey Avoth*, translated by Paul Forchheimer (New York; Feldheim Publishers, 1983), p. 112.
212. Maimonides, *Mishneh Torah*, pp. 17-18.
213. *Ibid.*, p. 17.
214. *Ibid.*, p. 14.
215. *Ibid.*, p. 27.
216. *Ibid.*, p. 19.
217. Maimonides, *Guide*, p. 46.
218. Maimonides, *Mishneh Torah*, p. 231.
219. Spero, pp. 75-76.
220. Jacobs, p. 93.
221. *Ibid.*, p. 106.

Part Four. Nuggets of Wisdom from Modern Jewish Thinkers

Note to Part Four, Luzzatto quotation. Moses Hayyim Luzzatto, *Mesillat Yesharim: The Path of the Upright*, translated and edited by Mordecai M. Kaplan (Philadelphia: The Jewish Publication Society of America, 1966), p. 8.

Note to Part Four, Franck citation. *A Philosopher's Harvest: The Philosophical Papers of Isaac Franck*, edited by William Gerber (Washington: Georgetown University Press, 1988), p. 95.

222. *Spinoza's Ethics and "De Intellectus Emendatione,"* translated by A. Boyle (London: J. M. Dent & Sons, and New York: E. P. Dutton & Co., Everyman's Library, 1925), p. 32.
223. *Ibid.*, p. 81.
224. *Ibid.*, p. 176.

225. *The Chief Works of Benedict de Spinoza*, translated by R. H. M. Elwes (New York: Dover Publications, two volumes, 1955), vol. 1, p. 83.

226. *Ibid.*, p. 82.

227. Moses Hayyim Luzzatto, *Derech haShem, The Way of God, and Ma'amar ha Ikkarim, An Essay on Fundamentals*, translated by Aryeh Kaplan (New York: Feldheim Publishers, 1981), p. 167.

228. Max Born, *Natural Philosophy of Cause and Chance* (Oxford: Clarendon Press, 1949), p. 122.

229. Heinz R. Pagels, *Perfect Symmetry: The Search for the Beginning of Time* (New York: Simon and Schuster, 1985), p. 21.

230. Albert Einstein, *The World As I See It*, translated by Alan Harris (New York: Covici-Friede, 1934), p. 242.

231. *Ibid.*, pp. 267-268.

232. Robert C. Baldwin and James A. S. McPeek (editors), *An Introduction to Philosophy Through Literature* (New York: The Ronald Press Co., 1950), p. 34.

233. Martin Buber, *Ten Rungs: Hasidic Sayings* (New York: Schocken Books, 1962), p. 15.

234. *Spinoza's Ethics*, pp. 1, 8-9.

235. Milton Steinberg, *Anatomy of Faith* (New York: Harcourt Brace Jovanovich, 1960), p. 89.

236. *Ibid.*, pp. 89-90.

237. *Ibid.*, pp. 90-91.

238. *Spinoza's Ethics* p. 159.

239. *Ibid.*, p. 192.

240. Franz Rosenzweig, *The Star of Redemption*, translated by William W. Hall (Boston: Beacon Press, 1972), p. 23.

241. David Baumgardt, "Maimonides: Religion as Poetic Truth," *Commentary*, vol. 18, November 1954, p. 445.

242. Charles C. Albertson (editor), *Lyra Mysica: An Anthology of Mystical Verse* (New York: The Macmillan Co., 1932), pp. 362-363.

243. *Ibid.*, p. 363-364.

244. Martin Buber, *The Way of Man According to the Teaching of Hasidism* (New York: The Citadel Press, 1966), p. 41.

245. Sidney Greenberg (editor), *A Modern Treasury of Jewish Thoughts* (New York: Thomas Yoseloff, 1960), p. 73.

246. *Spinoza's Ethics*, p. 39.

247. *Reason and Hope: Selections from the Jewish Writings of Hermann Cohen*, translated by Eva Jospe (New York: W. W. Norton and Co., 1971), p. 83.

248. *Dynamic Judaism: The Essential Writings of Mortimer M. Kaplan,* edited by Emanuel S. Goldsmith and Mel Scult (New York: Reconstructionist Press, 1985), p. 75.

249. Mordecai Kaplan, *Questions Jews Ask: Reconstructionist Answers* (New York: The Reconstructionist Press, 1956), p. 129.

250. Nancy Ross (editor), *The World of Zen: An East-West Anthology* (New York: Random House, 1960), p. 281.

251. Joseph B. Soloveitchik, *The Lonely Man of Faith* (New York: Doubleday, 1992), p. 22.

252. *Ibid.,* p. 23.

253. Emmanuel Levinas, *Nine Talmudic Readings,* translated by Annette Aronowicz (Bloomington, Ind.: Indiana University Press, 1990), pp. 14-15.

254. Emil L. Fackenheim, *Quest for Past and Future: Essays in Jewish Theology* (Bloomington, Ind.: Indiana University Press, 1968), pp. 163-164.

255. Nahum N. Glatzer (editor), *In Time and Eternity: A Jewish Reader* (New York: Schocken Books, 1946), p. 108.

256. Leo Baeck, *The Essence of Judaism* (New York: Schocken Books, 1961), p. 119.

257. Abraham J. Heschel, *Who Is Man?* (Stanford, Calif.: Stanford University Press, 1965), p. 73.

258. *Ibid.,* p. 112.

259. *Ibid.,* p. 119.

260. *Ibid.*

261. *Ibid.,* p. 68.

262. *Spinoza's Ethics,* p. 210.

263. Greenberg, p. 67.

264. George Seldes (editor), *The Great Quotations* (New York: Ballantine Books, 1985), p. 120.

265. Leonard J. Emmerglick, *Climbing the Celestial Ladder* (Coral Gables, Fla.: Tree of Life Books, 1989), p. 6.

266. William Gerber, *Pathways to a More Satisfying Life* (New York: Peter Lang Publishing, 1990), p. 82.

267. Elie Wiesel and Philippe-Michaël de Saint-Cheron, *Evil and Exile,* translated by Jon Rothschild (Notre Dame, Ind.: University of Notre Dame Press, 1990), p. 11.

268. *Ibid.,*

269. *Ibid.,* p. 12.

270. Rosenzweig, p. 229.

271. Edwin C. Johnson, *The Myth of the Great Secret: A Search for Spiritual Meaning in the Face of Emptiness* (New York; William Morrow and Co., 1982), p. 197.

272. Harold Heifetz (editor), *Zen and Hasidism: The Similarities Between Two Spiritual Disciplines* (Wheaton, Ill.: The Theosophical Publishing House, 1978), p. 181.

273. Glatzer, *Modern Jewish Thought*, p. 71.

274. Sidney Greenberg (editor), *Light from Jewish Lamps: A Modern Treasury of Jewish Thoughts* (Northvale, N.J.: Jason Aronson, 1986), p. 107.

275. *Ibid.*, p. 115.

276. *Ibid.*, p. 110.

277. *Ibid.*, p. 102.

278. *Ibid.*, p. 113.

279. *Reason and Hope*, p. 72.

280. *Ibid.*, p. 74.

281. Joseph H. Hertz (editor), *A Book of Jewish Thoughts* (New York: National Jewish Welfare Board, abridged edition, 1943), p. 49.

282. *Ibid.*, p. 42.

283. Heschel, p. 64.

284. *Ibid.*, p. 42.

285. Sidney Hook, *Convictions*, edited by Paul Kurtz (Buffalo, N.Y.: Prometheus Books, 1990), p. 61.

286. Wiesel and Saint-Cheron, p. 19.

287. *Spinoza's Ethics*, p. 174.

288. *Ibid.*, p. 88.

289. Philip Birnbaum (editor), *The New Treasury of Judaism* (New York: Sanhedrin Press, 1977), p. 417.

290. Gerber, p. 134.

291. *Ibid.*, p. 366.

292. Glatzer, *In Time and Eternity*, p. 113.

293. Gerber, p. 184.

294. Glatzer, p. 61.

295. Birnbaum, p. 429.

296. *Ibid.*, p. 430.

297. *Ibid.*, p. 431.

298. Buber, *Ten Rungs*, p. 165.

299. Nahum N. Glatzer (editor), *The Judaic Tradition* (New York: Behrman House, 1969), pp. 385-386.

300. Birnbaum, p. 407.

301. *A Shestov Anthology*, edited by Bernard Martin (Athens, Ohio: Ohio University Press, 1970), p. 72.

302. *The Writings of Martin Buber*, edited by Will Herberg (New York: Meridian Books, 1960), p. 55.

303. *Ibid.*, p. 60.

304. Heschel, p. 61.

305. *Ibid.*

306. Einstein, p. 237.

307. Wiesel and Saint-Cheron, p. 16.

308. Gerber, p. 118.

309. Glatzer, p. 607.

310. *Ibid.*, p. 331.

311. *Spinoza's Ethics*, p. 213.

312. *Reason and Hope* p. 85.

313. Leo Shestov, *All Things Are Possible, and Penultimate Words and Other Essays*, the former translated by S. S. Koteliansky and the latter by an anonymous translator (Athens, Ohio: Ohio University Press, 1977), p. 10.

314. *Jerusalem and Other Writings by Moses Mendelssohn*, translated by Alfred Jospe (New York: Schocken Books, 1969), p. 115.

315. *The New Republic*, vol. 202, April 2, 1990, p. 41.

316. *Judaism Eternal: Selected Essays from the Writings of Rabbi Samson Raphael Hirsch*, translated by Isidor Grunfeld (London: The Soncino Press, two volumes, 1956), vol. 1, p. 3.

317. Nathan and Maryann Ausubel (editors), *A Treasury of Jewish Poetry* (New York: Crown Publishers, 1957), p. 96.

318. Mortimer J. Adler and Charles Van Doren (editors), *Great Treasury of Western Thought* (New York: R. R. Bowker Co., 1977), p. 1,289.

319. *Ibid.*

320. *Reason and Hope*, p. 71.

321. *Ibid.*, p. 121.

322. Glatzer, *The Judaic Tradition*, p. 785.

323. *Ibid.*, p. 786.

324. Horace M. Kallen, *Judaism at Bay* (New York: Arno Press, 1972), p. 8.

325. *Ibid.*, p. 9.

326. Hertz, p. 3.

327. *Ibid.*, p. 61.

328. Glatzer, *Modern Jewish Thought*, p. 173.

329. *Ibid.*, p. 168.

INDEX OF AUTHORS
(AND ANONYMOUS DOCUMENTS) QUOTED

NOTE: Numbers shown here are quotation numbers, not page numbers.

ABOUT THE AUTHOR

William Gerber is a retired civil servant, who coordinated the preparation of social science data and analyses required for policy determination in the U.S. Departments of State and Labor. In addition, he served as a Consultant to the Harvard University Program on Technology and Society and composed balanced studies of disputed public issues for a national news agency which distributed the studies to opinion-makers in the print and electronic media.

Having earned a Ph.D. in philosophy at Columbia University, he taught philosophy classes at the University of Maryland for ten years, was secretary of the Washington Philosophy Club for twenty-five years, presented papers on controversial topics at international philosophical conferences in a dozen countries, and served on the international editorial board of the eight-volume *Encyclopedia of Philosophy*.

His book on serenity was made the basis of university seminars, an audiotape, etc., which drew wide attention. His book *The Mind of India*, published and reprinted in the United States, was re-issued after a quarter-century by a publisher in India.

VALUE INQUIRY BOOK SERIES

VIBS

1. Noel Balzer, **The Human Being as a Logical Thinker.**

2. Archie J. Bahm, **Axiology: The Science of Values.**

3. H. P. P. (Hennie) Lötter, **Justice for an Unjust Society.**

4. H. G. Callaway, **Context for Meaning and Analysis: A Critical Study in the Philosophy of Language.**

5. Benjamin S. Llamzon, **A Humane Case for Moral Intuition.**

6. James R. Watson, **Between Auschwitz and Tradition: Postmodern Reflections on the Task of Thinking.** A volume in **Holocaust and Genocide Studies.**

7. Robert S. Hartman, **Freedom to Live: The Robert Hartman Story,** edited by Arthur R. Ellis. A volume in **Hartman Institute Axiology Studies.**

8. Archie J. Bahm, **Ethics: The Science of Oughtness.**

9. George David Miller, **An Idiosyncratic Ethics; Or, the Lauramachean Ethics.**

10. Joseph P. DeMarco, **A Coherence Theory in Ethics.**

11. Frank G. Forrest, **Valuemetrics^ℵ: The Science of Personal and Professional Ethics.** A volume in **Hartman Institute Axiology Studies.**